FISHES

The giant devil ray can measure more than 5.2m(17ft) from
wing-tip to wing-tip and weigh over 1,360kg(3,000lb).

The fossilized remains of a bony fish, a relative of
the sunfishes, found in South American fresh waters.

NATURE FACTS

FISHES

LEN CACUTT

Grange
BOOKS

Published by Grange Books
An imprint of Grange Books Limited
The Grange
Grange Yard
London
SE1 3AG

Reprinted 1993
CLB 2591
© 1992 CLB Publishing, Godalming, Surrey
All rights reserved
Printed and bound in Italy by New Interlitho
ISBN 1-85627-334-2

The Author

For over 25 years, Len Cacutt has been engaged in every form of angling journalism, but over this period his interest in fishes and their evolution and conservation has overtaken his long participation in the sport of angling. He was founder-editor of *Angler's Mail* and has edited and compiled many angling magazines, books and encyclopaedias. He is a life member of the Freshwater Biological Association. In addition to his long involvement in all aspects of fishes and fishing, Len has pursued a broad range of interests in military and aviation history, mineralogy and geology, and has published books and articles on all these topics.

Credits

Edited and designed: Ideas into Print, Geoff Rogers and Stuart Watkinson
Layouts: Stuart Watkinson and Stonecastle Graphics Ltd.
Picture Editors: Annette Lerner, John Kaprielian
Photographs: Photo Researchers Inc., New York
Commissioning Editor: Andrew Preston
Production: Ruth Arthur, Sally Connolly, David Proffit, Andrew Whitelaw
Director of Production: Gerald Hughes
Typesetting: Ideas into Print
Colour Separations: Scantrans Pte. Ltd., Singapore

Gaudy clownfishes live in close harmony with sea anemones, immune from the effect of their deadly stinging tentacles.

CONTENTS

What is a fish?

Fishes are small-brained, cold-blooded animals with a skeleton of hard bones or soft cartilage, with paired or single fins and which breathe by means of gills that extract oxygen from the water in which they live. This description fits all fishes, from the parasitic lampreys and hagfishes, to the sharks and rays, and the vast number of ray- and spiny-finned fishes that abound in fresh and salt water. The shape, size, colour and habits of fishes vary enormously. Some, such as the Sargassofish, look more like a floating bunch of seaweed than a fish, while others look more like snakes. There are fishes that can produce 500-volt electric shocks, not fatal to man but deadly to prey animals that come too close. A few fishes have poisonous spines and gill-covers that can inflict very painful wounds to man and are fatal to many aquatic animals. Some eat poisonous plant material and pass a killing illness called ciguatera to man. All are true fishes.

The humpback whale's flat, boneless tail is horizontal, but in fishes the tailfin is vertical. The whale has very long flippers, which are equivalent to the pectoral fins of fishes.

Tailfin

A fish with many names: leopard, coral cod, coral trout, blue spot, rock cod, vermilion sea bass - and yet it is neither a cod nor a trout, but a sea perch, one of the vast number of spiny-finned sea fishes. Using its fins, the fish is able to manoeuvre easily among the corals of a tropical reef.

In the bony fishes, the fins are supported by rays, as seen in this anal fin. In sharks and similar fishes, the skeleton is a more flexible cartilage material.

Dolphins are members of the whale family and at first appear to be very similar to fish. Although they spend their entire lives in water, they do not have gills and do not lay eggs. They are air-breathing mammals that have successfully colonized the sea and fresh waters. Like land mammals, they produce live young and suckle them with milk.

Dorsal fin

This is a typical shape for a fish, with a pointed head and smoothly streamlined body. The tailfin provides forward thrust, the dorsal and anal fins prevent rolling, while the pelvic and pectoral fins are used for steering and braking.

The large mouth indicates that this fish is a predator, feeding on creatures of the reefs. Many fishes have a much less aggressive lifestyle and have small mouths for reaching between rock crevices to pick off plant fragments.

Anal fin

Pectoral fins
(Pelvic fins hidden)

Not all animals that live in water are fishes, even though some are known as starfishes, crayfishes and shellfishes. Salt and fresh waters hold huge numbers of animals without backbones - invertebrates - some with single or paired shells, some with a hard body covering, such as crabs and lobsters, while others are simple, soft-bodied creatures, such as worms and jellyfish. All these animals live their lives under water using gills to remove the oxygen they need to sustain life, but they are not fishes.

Although resembling fish in general shape and equipped with fins, whales, porpoises and dolphins are warm-blooded mammals with comparatively large brains. Their boneless tailfins are horizontal, not vertical like those in fishes and their ancestors developed tailfins for the same reason that the fishes did, to propel their bodies efficiently through the water. These mammals breathe air, but some can hold their breath for over an hour as they dive deeply in the ocean.

In shape, size and colour, the fishes present a vast spectrum. Some fish are gorgeous, not a few repulsive. Many are dangerous to man as well as to other fishes, whereas some make fine pets. The largest fish is the whale shark at up to 12m (about 40ft) long and the smallest is the pygmy goby at 11mm(0.43in) long - probably the smallest vertebrate animal. There is a clue to this tremendous diversity among the fishes, for life began in water. There was life in the sea when the land was an endless vista of barren rock and lava flows. No wonder then that fishes have such a variety of form and lifestyles - after all, they have had a head start of 400 million years.

The first fishes

How did fishes evolve? The answer may be found in a thin layer of 550-million-year-old rock high in the Canadian Rockies, called the Burgess Shale. Among fossils of strange creatures with no relatives living today there is a 7.5cm(3in)-long wormlike creature with a stiff rod running along its back, supporting a nerve cord and the zig-zag bands of muscle familiar to us in modern fishes. In the sand of the seabed today there lives a primitive fish called the lancelet, or amphioxus, that still has many characteristics of that ancient but beautifully preserved fossil.

Unfortunately, scientists looking for 'missing links' have found few clues to explain how today's main groups of fishes arose. One possible reason is that the very earliest fishes lived in fresh water, where very few fossils were formed in the associated rocks. Nevertheless, it is clear that the first backboned fishes lived 400 million years ago. They had circular, jawless mouths and fed by sucking water through this small orifice and taking whatever food particles it contained. Their

fossils were first found in Scotland and Norway, in a layer of rocks called the Old Red Sandstone. They had armoured bodies and no fins. Some swam in fresh water and perhaps migrated to the sea to breed. These fishes were the ancestors of the jawless lampreys and hagfishes, which today attach themselves to living fishes by their fixed, circular mouths. It took millions of years for fishes to develop hinged jaws - probably arising from bones that support the gills - and lose much of the head and body armour. Jaws were a giant step forward for animals with backbones -

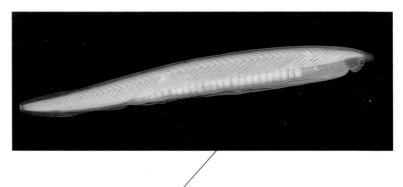

Fishes developed from animals like this amphioxus. It has no jaws, no bones and no fins, but has a general fishlike shape, lies buried in sand and extracts oxygen from the water.

Encased in armoured plates and scales, the cephalaspids of 400 million years ago bore a clear resemblance to modern fishes. The two eyes close together on top of the head could only look straight up, however, and there is the suggestion of a third, so-called 'pineal eye', between the two ordinary ones.

especially for feeding – and so these fishes quickly replaced the former armoured kinds. All the major groups of fishes we see in today's rivers and seas had their beginnings in the ancient Old Red Sandstone. These are the strange jawless lampreys and hagfishes, the sharks and rays, and the bony fishes – by far the largest group. It was once thought that sharks and rays, fishes with a skeleton made of flexible cartilage, were more 'primitive' than fishes with hard bones. But evidence shows that bone developed first and the ancestors of today's sharks had proper bony skeletons.

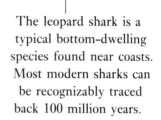

The leopard shark is a typical bottom-dwelling species found near coasts. Most modern sharks can be recognizably traced back 100 million years.

The mouth of the jawless cephalaspids was a small orifice beneath the bony shield covering the head.

These are gill pouches each side of the mouth.

The heterocercal tail is a primitive feature still seen in sharks today. The upper lobe is bigger than the lower one and tends to force the head down when swung from side to side.

Fossils of early bony fishes are abundant and, if well preserved, their structures can be closely examined. From the rock around fossilized bones we can find out whether the fish lived in fresh or salt water.

13

How fishes live

Fishes cannot live without oxygen but, with one or two exceptions, neither can they live out of water. Therefore, they have developed a system of extracting oxygen from water. When you watch a goldfish, you can see its gill-covers moving steadily in and out as it draws water in through the mouth and out over the fine gill membranes. A countercurrent blood flow through the gills makes the extraction of oxygen from the water - and the release of carbon dioxide into it - an efficient process.

Living in water needs a finely tuned set of sense organs. At the brightly lit surface, eyes are small, whereas in the depths or in nocturnal fish, the eyes are large so that they can collect every available glimmer of light. Predators need sharp vision, and the pike is one of the few fishes with binocular sight; both eyes look forward and the visual fields overlap. Most fishes have their eyes on either side of the head and it is difficult to imagine what their brain 'sees'. Most fish do not have eyelids, but sharks have a membrane that slides across the eye as it closes in on its kill. Many bony fishes have good colour vision. The senses of taste and smell in fishes tend to overlap. In water, taste is a reaction to a substance close to or actually touching the mouth, whereas the sense of smell enables fish to detect substances tainting the water at a distance. Sharks and piranhas react very

The pike has all the attributes of an efficient predator: keen eyesight for assessing distance, strong jaws with sharp teeth for grasping prey, and a long body and muscular tailfin for making sudden lunges from its hiding place among the weeds.

The rainbow trout is a classic fish shape, with all the fins typical of these highly adapted underwater creatures. Rainbows include invertebrates in their varied diet.

quickly to small amounts of blood in the water. Marine fishes are in danger of drying out because water tends to flow out of their bodies into the relatively strong solution of sea water surrounding them. To counteract this, they constantly drink sea water and produce small amounts of concentrated urine. They also actively eliminate excess salts through the gills. Freshwater fishes face the prospect of becoming waterlogged as pure water

...hes and man

This Roman mosaic of men fishing dates from the second century A.D. They used baited hooks, nets and spears, including tridents. One favourite addition to a Roman meal was fish sauce, imported in the shapely jars found in the many wrecks dating from that period.

Man has devised many methods of catching fish. This stilt fisher in Sri Lanka may be mimicking wading birds that fish in thick mudflats.

Man and fish share a long association, not only because both have evolved from the ...me ancestor living over 400 million years ago, ...t also because man began catching fish a ...illion years ago. He trapped them, scooped ...em out and even fashioned hooks from flint and ...one to catch them, eating them raw before he ...sed fire to cook food. Now, his predations are ...uch more successful. His deepsea trawlers have ...ets capable of taking vast quantities of food fish, ...nd this harvesting continues to the extent that ...ome commercially valuable fishes are in danger ...f extinction. This has happened in spite of a ...learned professor who, in 1883, gave his opinion that the fishes were inexhaustible; that nothing we could do would affect their numbers!

The fishes in fresh water largely escape this serious commercial threat, but not entirely. Considerable numbers of carp and trout are reared for the table, but this artificial production does not affect the wild populations, whose main threat is from sportfishing, which has steadily increased since the end of World War Two.

Sportfishing falls into the main categories of sea and freshwater fishing. The sea angler fishes from the shore or from boats. When fishing with strong tackle and for powerful species, such as marlin, this is 'deepsea game fishing'; from small boats, it is 'inshore fishing'. Sea angling is also carried out from beaches, rocks, piers and harbour walls; in fact, from any place where a baited hook can be cast and where fish are likely to rise to it. Many species of sea fish are sought

constantly seeps into their bodies. Their kidneys retain salts and produce large amounts of weak urine. Fishes that migrate between fresh and salt water adjust their 'water management systems' as they pass from one environment to the other.

Sound travels well in water and, although fishes have no vocal organs as such, there are fishes capable of producing considerable sounds, mostly by vibrating internal muscles. Fishes do not have external ears, but they do have inner ear capsules that contain balance sensors and in some fishes provide a degree of hearing, especially in those that can respond to vibrations picked up by the swimbladder. Fishes also have a system of canals on the head and down the flanks - the lateral line system - that can detect vibrations.

The streamlined shape and muscular tailfin of many fishes allow them to swim very fast, either to avoid predators or to chase prey. The paired fins act like paddles to steer them through the water.

Pressure sensors in the lateral line system enable fish to detect vibrations in the water, thus helping them to find food, and avoid predators and obstacles.

Pacific salmon have been known to travel 3,300km(2,250 miles) upstream to deposit and fertilize eggs. Evidence shows that they may use a combination of smell and magnetism to navigate their way from the sea.

The large nostrils of the piranha reflect its dependence on detecting the faintest traces of blood in the water to alert it to potential food.

The flow of water over the gills, which take up oxygen and release carbon dioxide, is maintained by movement of the gill-covers and the jaws, hence the constant opening and closing of the mouth.

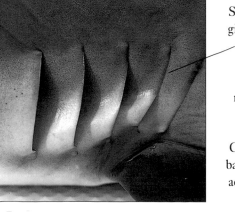

Sharks and rays have exposed gill slits not covered by a gill-cover. When the shark is swimming, oxygen-bearing water enters through the mouth. At rest, the gill slits pump water over the gills.

Catfishes have long, sensitive barbels around the mouth that act as touch and taste sensors in murky waters.

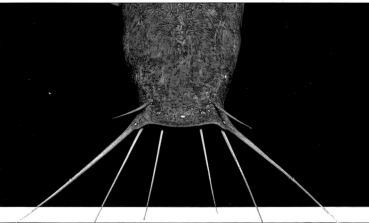

How fishes reproduce

Anyone who can afford caviar knows that it comes from a fish, but most fish roe makes very good eating for the simple reason that, like all eggs, it is full of goodness. Not all fishes release eggs; in some sharks the eggs are retained inside the female and the young are born alive with yolk-sacs attached, in others the young are enclosed in sturdy, translucent egg capsules. Livebearing also occurs to various degrees in some other fishes, including the popular guppies, mollies, platies and swordtails familiar to aquarists. Most livebearing fishes employ a form of internal fertilization, with modified fins on the males being used to deposit sperm within the females body close to the eggs.

There is little courtship among most fishes, and at spawning times they generally congregate in huge shoals, the females releasing clouds of eggs that the males fertilize with their sperm (called milt) and in most cases the eggs are then left to

Tendrils at the four corners of the eggcase get tangled up with weed fronds and hide it from the eyes of predators.

Dogfishes - small sharks - produce eggs in horny cases within which the embryo develops, living off the large, rich yolk until it is able to exist independently. The capsule is composed of keratin, the material that makes birds' claws hard.

A male lesser spotted dogfish curls itself around the female during mating.

Unlike most fishes, sharks actually copulate. While entwined with the female, the male introduces one of two bony claspers through which sperm flows.

Parental care is sometimes seen in fishes. Cichlids will shepherd large groups of young with apparent concern. Here, tiny discus fry stay close to the parents, feeding on the mucus coating their flanks.

The male stickleback creates a nest by burrowing a tunnel through plant debris and then coaxes a female inside, where the eggs are laid and fertilized.

take their chances. Some fish deposit the eggs on the bottom, while others eject them to float on the surface of the water. The number of eggs released by some fishes is enormous, a 1.5m(5ft) ling was found to have over 28 million eggs in its body and a 7.2kg(16.5lb) carp is recorded as carrying two million eggs. As they lie on the bottom or are taken along by wind and current on the surface, eggs are subject to severe predation, but the huge numbers released ensure that there will always be another generation.

Where few eggs are produced, they are either hidden or there is a measure of parental care and protection from predators. In mouthbrooding cichlids, the fertilized eggs are carried in the mouth of the female and even after hatching the tiny young stay close and scuttle back into her mouth at the first sign of danger. Both sexes of a

small South American freshwater fish, spraying characin, leap together from th and leave fertilized eggs on an overhang the male keeping them wet by regularly the leaf. When the eggs hatch, the fry si drop into the water below.

The majority of fishes have simple sexua organs that enable them to switch easily fr being female to male. Some tropical marine have both sets of sexual organs. The Amaz molly is found only as a female, the species reproduced by having its eggs fertilized by t male of a closely related species, but the eggs produce females only. The reason for this is thought to be the result of some long past hybridization. Minnows and guppies are know change from female to male in late adulthood, probably as a natural form of population contro

by anglers, from large shark, marlin, barracuda, groupers and swordfish down to members of the cod family, flatfishes, skates and smaller species.

Freshwater fishing is divided into 'game fishing' for salmon and trout with artificial fly or lure, and 'coarse fishing' for the carp family, perch, pike and freshwater eel. Fly fishermen take salmon from the rivers in which they run to spawn and wild trout from rivers and lakes. Many trout are now bred for fishing purposes and released into reservoirs, and this mode of trout fishing has become very popular.

Thus, sadly, the greatest danger to fishes, even though they have their own predators, is man. Primitive man found that they were edible and he has eaten them ever since. But today he harvests them from the water in such huge quantities that for many their existence is threatened. He uses fishing tackle to catch them as a form of sporting activity; he breeds them for this purpose and for keeping as pets in aquariums. Man's factories need water so he takes it from the rivers and seas and uses it to cool his machinery. When that water returns to its

source much of it is hot and polluted - and lethal to fish life. Agriculture is being paid vast sums to produce food (which is often never eaten!) and does so by employing many harmful chemicals; then it rains and the residue runs into the water. Slurry (liquid manure from pigs and cattle), and silage (liquefied cattle-feed) is lethal and percolates into rivers and streams to kill off fish over large areas as it runs downstream. Now, he is polluting the atmosphere with emissions from power stations and 'acid rain' reacts with aluminium in the soil and prevents fish breeding. There are many ways to spoil the fishes' environment - and we use them all.

A small commercial fishing boat in Cook Inlet, Gulf of Alaska. Fish movement may be detected from the tower.

An angler wading in the cold, spring-fed Metolius River, Central Oregon, USA. He is fishing for the rainbow trout for which this tributary of the Deschutes River is noted.

In the dinghy, a crewman checks the buoys that support the nets. These waters are prolific with Coho and chinook salmon, and large halibut weighing up to 45kg(100 lb).

Mythical monsters

This ichthyosaur, a 'fish-reptile' with a sharklike tail, hunted in ancient seas over 150 million years ago.

If reptiles such as this plesiosaur still exist, it will be in the ocean depths. Mariners tell of craft being threatened by long-necked monsters.

Old maps and charts are often decorated with mythical monsters of the sea, some recognizable, some straight off the science fiction shelves, and sailors' diaries often contain vivid descriptions of monsters that rose from the depths. Who is to say that these serious, worldly-wise seamen were making up all these tales when the rest of their accounts can be seen to be accurate? Sea serpents, while not fishes, have been described in detail, as huge creatures clinging to ships and overturning them. There are certainly giant squids living in deep water that if brought to the surface by storms or undersea earthquake activity would frighten the life out of any sailor. Whales have been captured bearing the weals left by the clutching tentacles of huge squid or cuttlefish. One 'sea serpent' measuring 17m(56ft) long and cast up on the shores of the Orkney Isles north of Scotland early in the nineteenth century seems to have been a dead ribbonfish, which can approach that length. In 1922 a gigantic creature about 30m(100ft) swam into the harbour at Cristobal, Panama. It was shot with machine guns and bombed to pieces - but never identified.

The manatee does not look particularly human, but year after year at sea can do strange things to the imagination. Related to the dugongs, or sea cows, these mammals may have been the source of the mythical mermaid stories brought back from long voyages.

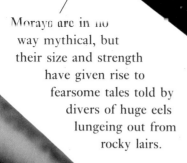

Morays are in no way mythical, but their size and strength have given rise to fearsome tales told by divers of huge eels lungeing out from rocky lairs.

❏ Raining 'cats and dogs' has long been a popular description of severe downpours, but it certainly has rained fishes on occasion. Powerful winds and waterspouts can suck huge amounts of water from the sea, along with any fishes and other creatures light enough to be lifted up by the suction created as the winds circle at high speeds. When released over land as rain, the water and its accompanying 'fish shower' must seem puzzling and 'mythical' to many people.

❏ In 1905, two naturalists reported sighting a creature in the sea off Brazil. The reptilian head on a 2m(6.5ft)-long neck reared out of the sea, before it sank out of sight. The report was published in the Proceedings of the Royal Society of London, a well-respected publication.

Sturgeons – fish from the past

With their knobbly armoured bodies that make them look like fish dinosaurs, the sturgeons reflect their links with the ancient past. In fact, these fishes are the descendants of a long-extinct group that lived 130 million years ago. One clue to their long ancestry is the way the backbone runs up into the upper lobe of the tail, a common feature in primitive fishes; modern fishes have backbones that continue only up to the front of the tailfin. The primitive body has a single or sometimes two rows of armoured plates along the flanks, but the fins have no bony support - in fact, the whole skeleton is made of cartilage. The head is covered by more heavy plates, and long barbels protrude between the front of the snout and the fixed, semi-circular mouth. The underslung mouth shows that this fish feeds on the bottom, using its turned-up snout, or 'nose', to stir up the mud and expose likely prey in the shape of worms, molluscs, crustaceans and even small fishes.

Small, underslung and protrusible, the mouth of the Atlantic sturgeon has two pairs of sensory feelers, aids to finding small invertebrate foods in the rivers and the sea.

The lake sturgeon has longer mouth feelers than other species and the armoured plates along its sides are more massive. Unfortunately, over-fishing and pollution have made it a rare species today.

The sturdy, streamlined snout is ideal for rooting about in the bottom sediment for food.

Sturgeons are found only in the Northern Hemisphere, where some of the 25 species live entirely in fresh water, while others spawn in fresh water and then migrate to the sea.

The upturned snout and fringed feelers are typical of this small sturgeon, *Acipenser sturio*.

The larger upper lobe tends to drive the head of the fish downwards.

Here, the vertebrae can be seen running along the body and up into the tail, a condition known as heterocercal.

❑ Sturgeons are among the largest fishes; the beluga can reach a length of 8m(26.2ft). One beluga captured in 1922 weighed 1,220kg(2,690lb); the head alone weighed 288kg(635lb)! A female weighing 246kg(542lb) was found to be carrying nearly 8,000,000 eggs. Female beluga can live for 100 years.

❑ Known as caviar, (from the Turkish 'khavyar', meaning 'bearing eggs'), the sturgeon's roe has been eaten since the thirteenth century. Given the fish's declining numbers, this delicacy can only become more expensive; clearly, conservation measures are long overdue.

❑ The beluga sturgeon migrates from the Black and Caspian Seas to spawn upriver, producing the largest eggs and thus the most desirable caviar.

❑ The sterlet is small enough to be kept in an aquarium.

❑ Except for the Tsars, few Europeans have tasted the famed 'gold' caviar of the sterlet, one of the smaller sturgeons that grows up to about 120cm(48in) in length. Before World War 1, this rare delicacy was kept only for the Russian Imperial Court.

❑ Apart from caviar, sturgeons also provide isinglass, a gelatinous material obtained from the swimbladder and used as an adhesive.

Face to face with a living fossil

In ancient rocks lie the fossilized remains of a strange fish with fleshy, tassel-like fins, rather like legs with fins instead of feet. This was a freshwater fish, but millions of years ago climatic conditions and severe changes in the environment drove it into the seas. It was thought that this fish - the coelacanth - was extinct, only to be seen as a fossil. This was the situation until 1938, when a fisherman hauling in his nets off East London, South Africa, found a strange, blue-scaled fish among his usual catch. By the time he had brought it ashore, the tropical sun had done its work and the very smelly carcass was hurriedly cleaned and stuffed. When it was shown to a zoologist, he had a shock - he never imagined he would ever see the actual body of a coelacanth! Since then, further specimens have been caught off the east coast of South Africa. Now this 1.8m(6ft)-long 'living fossil' has been carefully studied and the secrets of its ancient body revealed.

Scientists in deep-diving submersibles have observed the coelacanth in its own habitat down to 274m(900ft) in the Indian Ocean.

Eggs the size of a tennis ball were found in one female and live embryos in another, evidence that this fish produces living young.

The vertebrae in the coelacanth backbone extend into the tailfin, which has a strange three-lobed shape.

The scaly fins are mounted on stalks that allow more movement than modern fish.

The paddlefish is another living fossil. It can grow up to 2.2m(7ft 3in) long, and one specimen weighed 91kg(200lb). It uses the paddle to stir up mud to release clouds of plankton.

The primitive bowfin's swimbladder is connected to its throat, enabling the fish to breathe air in conditions where other fish would die.

Like the coelacanth, the bowfin is the sole survivor of an ancient group of fishes that were widespread many millions of years ago. The bowfin hunts small fishes in clear river waters.

A mysterious organ has been found in the nose of the coelacanth. On each side of the head there are three mucus-filled tubes ending at the surface of the skin. It seems not to be involved with the sense of smell.

❑ The ancient relatives of the paddlefish, another primitive fish, had strong bones, but today the paddlefish has a soft cartilaginous skeleton and a sharklike tail. So this fish, once widespread, but now found only in the Mississippi River system, has degenerated in its structure. Its most distinctive feature is the long, flat, paddle-shaped bill, equipped with many sensitive organs that allow the paddlefish to locate the huge number of tiny organisms that it filters from the water through close-set gill rakers in the mouth.

❑ The natives of Madagascar (shown above), where the coelacanth was first seen by scientists, called it *kombessa* and had been eating it as a food fish for years!

❑ The snakelike frilled shark is a very primitive deepwater shark, the sole remaining member of a large family that lived 15 million years ago.

❑ The long history of the bowfin, or mudfish, can be seen in its skeleton, especially the jaws, which still retain very primitive features.

Manta rays – gentle giants of the ocean

Ponderous but graceful, the manta flaps serenely through the seas, feeding as it goes.

Despite their formidable appearance, the manta rays are not a threat to man. The cloak shape of the body accounts for the name manta (meaning 'cloak'), whereas the 'horns' each side of the mouth probably explain the alternative common name of 'devil fish'. The largest of these impressive and very graceful fishes, the giant devil ray, flaps serenely through the water on its huge wing-shaped pectoral fins. These fish can weigh up to 1,360kg(3,000lb) and measure 6.7m(22ft) across the wings. The giant devil ray, devil ray and pygmy devil ray have soft-boned skeletons typical of the skates and rays. Mantas feed by scooping quantities of floating planktonic animals - and occasionally larger fish - into their mouths, guided by the mobile fleshy horns on either side of the jaws. A trapped and terrified diver could well believe that the ray was acting aggressively when it was only attempting to swallow what seemed to it to be a large fish.

The 'wings' of the manta are very elongated and thickened pectoral fins, ideal for 'flying' through the water.

The manta is harmless, but a close inspection between the horns is not recommended.

There are no teeth in the upper jaw of the manta. The huge 'horns' (properly called cephalic fins) on either side of the mouth scoop up plankton, small marine animals and even fishes.

FACT FILE

❑ The large openings, called spiracles, on the heads of skates and rays are sometimes mistaken for eyes, but they are part of the fish's respiratory system.

❑ While not known to attack man deliberately, the devil ray has sometimes surfaced under fishing boats and overturned them. Mantas have been harpooned on occasion, but these fishes are so strong that lines often have to be cut to avoid the boat being pulled below the surface of the water.

❑ Some smaller rays give birth to live young, while others produce brownish transparent egg cases, popularly known as mermaids' purses, which are often washed ashore after the young rays have left them. When the eggs are dropped from the fish, long tendrils at each corner of the egg cases cling to weed fronds and hold the capsules near the seabed as they develop.

❑ Some large fishes do not have big babies, but the manta ray has been known to produce an embryo measuring 1.2m(4ft) wide and weighing up to12kg(28lb).

❑ The common skate, a member of a large family of skates and rays, can measure 2.4m(8ft) across the wings and has been aptly described as a swimming grand piano.

A pair of remoras accompany the manta, feeding on food particles from its mouth.

The eagle ray's head projects in front of the wings and there are no fleshy scoops around the mouth.

The manta cruises close to the tropical seabed in search of plankton. Its ancestors lived 70 million years ago.

The tales you hear about pikes

A huge folklore exists about the pike, most of it based on fact but distorted beyond belief. Reports of ducklings being pulled below the surface and swallowed can be believed, but what about the published tales of dogs being pulled in, of human feet and ankles being bitten by ravenous pike? Perhaps these claims are not surprising, given the pike's appearance and predatory behaviour. Its large, powerful jaws are armed with sharp doglike teeth and, as an aid to swallowing prey, there are three rows of smaller, backward-pointing teeth in the roof of the mouth. There is but one direction for a prey fish held in the pike's jaws - down its capacious throat. The pike has a powerful tailfin for quick, sudden propulsion, and the dorsal and anal fins are set well back along its long, muscular body. It lies in ambush, camouflaged in weedbeds, until its sensory system detects the approach of a fish. Its eyes focus like binoculars on its prey and only when the fish is within quick striking distance will the pike lunge forward at speed to grasp its food. Then it retreats to its lair, where it turns the prey and swallows it headfirst.

The pike will retreat to turn a captured fish headfirst before swallowing it.

The tailfin is ideal for making a sudden lunge from cover. One flick and the fish homes in on its prey.

Body markings vary between pike in rivers and lakes with different types of water. This 'jack' pike - a near perfect predator - weighs about 2.2kg(5lb).

The pike has forward-looking eyes that give it binocular vision, so it can judge the distance to its prey and make a quick and effective attack.

Grasped in the canines of the lower jaw, a prey fish is also pinned by three rows of small, sharp teeth in the roof of the mouth. These all point backwards.

Pelvic fins are used as brakes and for manoeuvring during an attack.

Lurking among clumps of weed, the pike can lie patiently in wait for an easy kill. There is no long chase involved, only a sudden lunge and closing of the jaws to grasp the prey. A swallowing action by muscles connected to bones supporting the gills moves the food down the throat.

❏ Fossil pike, perfectly preserved in rocks, are evidence that the species has changed little in the past 25 million years.

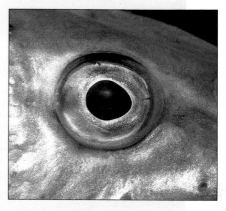

❏ From the prey's point of view it is easy to imagine that the cold eyes of a pike (shown above) homing in with its jaws just about to open can instill paralyzing fear.

❏ The legendary 'emperor's pike' caught in 1497 reputedly weighed 250kg(550lb), was almost 6m(20ft) long and carried a tag to 'prove' it was 260 years old!

❏ The Amur pike is found in the eastern USSR and grows to 114cm(45in). It is known to migrate, feeding in rivers and moving to lakes to spawn.

❏ In the Great Lakes of North America, the muskellunge once grew to 2.4m(8ft) and weighed over 45kg(100lb). It is still the largest pike, but now averages perhaps half that size. Muskellunge is a corruption of the Indian Ojibway name 'mas Kinononge' for 'ugly pike'.

Fishes with their own fishing rods

This tropical frogfish has a rodlike lure with tassels on the end.

Fishermen, sea mammals, birds and the grizzly bear are not the only creatures to go fishing; some fishes have themselves developed this ability and employ it very successfully. For example, the front spine of the anglerfish's dorsal fin has become elongated and hangs over the mouth with a 'bait' on the end that trembles irresistibly to entice prey fish within reach. When the prey is close enough, the anglerfish's great jaws jerk open in a flash and the inrush of water carries the small fish into its mouth. There are anglerfishes in the lakes of West Africa that do not have a twitching 'lure' but entice their prey by a light-producing organ in their mouths. Another anglerfish not only has a 'lure' on a 'rod' but the lure is equipped with hooks! The Indo-Pacific striped angler has developed a forked 'fishing rod'; another lives in the Sargasso Sea area of the Atlantic Ocean where, using prehensile fins, it clings to the fronds of weed that float about in huge clumps. It has no fishing rod but it certainly 'angles' as it waits, perfectly camouflaged, for likely prey fish to approach. The grotesque frogfishes, relatives of the anglerfishes, also go fishing. The success of 'lure fishing' is well shown by the discovery of ten 10cm(4in) fish stacked inside the distended stomach of an 18cm(7in)-long frogfish.

The anglerfish with fringed jaws agape lies in wait for prey.

The dorsal fins are festooned with fleshy tendrils. The front one acts as an enticing lure, as the fish twitches it over the camouflaged mouth.

The frogfishes have largely ceased to swim, crawling slowly about weed-covered rocks and corals, where they find perfect concealment.

Around the margin of the anglerfish's jaws there are curved teeth that fold back to allow prey fish to move down into the gullet.

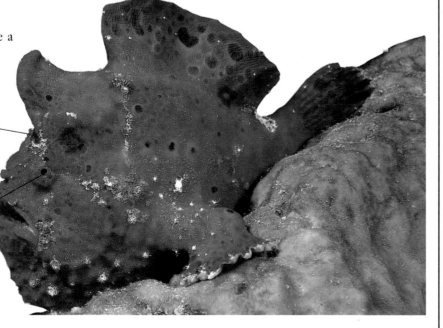

The loose envelope of skin, with its weedlike filaments and colour mimicry, provide total camouflage.

All the frogfishes have a rough skin covered with warty growths. The body shape is irregular and the lure is shorter than in the closely related anglerfishes.

The eye of the red frogfish is a black spot, much like others on the grotesque body.

FACT FILE

❏ Deepsea anglerfishes, as shown above, are found at depths of over 930m(3,000ft). In the darkness of the seabed, where these fishes live, their lure is luminous and situated on the end of an extended finray. It can be waggled and then retracted, bringing prey fish close enough to be engulfed as the fish suddenly opens its mouth.

❏ Off the American coast, from Newfoundland to North Carolina in the western Atlantic, the goosefish 'fishes' at depths of over 558m(1,800ft). This fish reaches 1.2m(4ft) long and can weigh 22.6kg(50lb). The goosefish, a US relative of the European anglerfishes, is so-called because of its habit of darting forward with its mouth open just like an angry - or hungry - goose.

❏ Diving birds, swimming close to the seabed, have been attracted by the anglerfish's moving 'lure' and suddenly found themselves swept into the lurking fish's cavernous jaws.

Clownfishes – safe within the deadliest embrace

The common clownfish, *Amphiprion ocellaris*, in the tentacles of its host anemone, *Heteractis malu*. They spell danger for any other fish.

These beautiful reef fishes have evolved a unique method of avoiding the cut and thrust of the 'kill or be killed' struggle beneath the waves. Instead of steering clear of danger, they have taken up residence in one of the most dangerous places of all! Quite simply, they have adapted to live among the stinging tentacles of sea anemones – a habitat that would paralyze other small fishes and make them easy prey to these beautiful but deadly invertebrates. Far from being harmed, clownfishes hovering near their host anemone are able to dart back into its 'welcoming' arms at the slightest hint of danger, remaining secure from predators that dare not pursue their cause any further. In fact, throughout their lives, clownfishes rarely stray much further than 1m(about 3ft) away from the anemone's protective embrace. They may also feed within the anemone's tentacles, scavenging for small crustaceans, algae and plankton that abound in the warm waters. What does the anemone gain in return? One theory is that the bright coloration of the clownfishes serves to ward off predators that threaten the anemone.

Aptly named, these tomato clownfishes nestle happily among the tentacles of their host sea anemone.

The beautiful salmon clownfish – a shy species found along the Great Barrier Reef.

Away from the protective tentacles, clownfishes are at risk and must seize food items swiftly.

❏ The name 'clownfish' is thought to have originated from the bright coloration and white stripes across the fish's body, which resemble the white greasepaint markings traditionally used by clowns.

❏ The clownfish is safe from the anemone's stinging tentacles because its skin is covered with a protective mucus that the anemone recognizes as part of its own body. Young clownfishes dash through the anemone's tentacles to pick up some of this 'camouflage' mucus.

❏ Clownfishes are likely to change sex as they mature. All are male at birth, but dominant fishes become female in later life. Pairs form a strong bond, with the female laying her eggs under the canopy of the anemone's guarding tentacles.

❏ On an evolutionary scale, sea anemones have a longer history than clownfishes, so the two species cannot have evolved together.

❏ The various species of clownfishes associate with particular species of anemone. Each type of clownfish tends to have a localized distribution, depending on the availability of suitable anemones. Spreading further afield is difficult for clownfishes, because when the fry hatch they stay close to the adults and are unlikely to survive if they are swept away from the shallow waters of the reef out into the open sea.

Remoras – fishes that stick to their friends

The name remora, meaning a 'hindrance', is an apt one for this group of fishes, which attach themselves to whales, turtles and porpoises, as well as to smooth-bodied fishes, such as sharks. Remoras, also known as shark suckers, have an oval 'disc' occupying the whole of the top of the head. This is formed from a modified ray of the dorsal fin. When the disc comes into contact with the flat skin of another fish, ridges inside the disc are raised, creating a powerful suction. Each remora species seems to prefer one particular host. As with many unusual changes in body and organs, the remora's sucking disc is a highly complex adaptation. The remora's way of life seems to compensate for its lack of stamina for independent travel. As it accompanies the host fish, the remora also cleans it of external parasites, which may be the remora's only source of nourishment. Even ships can be plagued by remoras; if the fish are present in large numbers, the effect of their combined bodies can impede the ship's passage.

A group of remoras at rest beneath the bulk of a manta ray. Much of their food consists of small crustaceans, called copepods, attached to the manta ray's gills.

Once attached to a host by its complex sucker, a remora is very difficult to remove, even when it dies.

A remora attached to a whitetip shark. It will cling onto the skin when the shark slows down or stops.

❏ The natives of Cuba used remoras to catch turtles by attaching a line to the fish's tail and releasing it in the water near the reptile. The remora would make for the turtle, just as it would to any suitable host, attach itself by its sucking disc and then both fish and turtle were pulled into the boat. This practice was first noted in a report published in the sixteenth century, but the story was dismissed as being too ridiculous!

❏ There are eight remora species; the largest is 90cm(36in) long and found in most tropical seas.

❏ Husbands in Madagascar wishing to keep their wives faithful cut a piece off a remora's suction disc and attach it to the lady's neck - hoping that the wife will stick to her husband!

❏ The remora stays attached to its host (as shown above) while moving about or at rest, releasing its suction-held grip to browse on the external parasites that infest many fishes. They also briefly leave the host to snap up any morsels of food dropped by it.

The cod family – familiar as food but not as fish

The cod fishes are widespread in the Northern Hemisphere, but few are found in southern waters. They are not usually regarded as predatory, yet they sweep across the seabed swallowing anything edible that fits into their large mouths - fish, crabs, shellfish and all kinds of human debris that sinks to the seabed. Most cods have one or more barbels on their mouths, which act as taste and tactile sensors. One member of the cod family - the hake - is particularly fierce, and is not averse to eating its own young as well as other cod relatives. As a commercially valuable fish, the hake has been seriously affected by overnetting; at one time fish weighing 11.3kg(25lb) were regularly brought ashore, but now the average size is less than half that. The same threat of overfishing applies to the cod itself. The arctic cod is found down to a depth of 730m(2,400ft) in the Atlantic and Pacific Oceans, right up to the edge of the polar icecap. It is food for seals, arctic foxes, polar bears, whales and even birds. The ling, found at similar depths, is an active predator from the Atlantic that grows to 20kg(45lb).

Most bottom-feeding fish, like this Atlantic cod, have one or more barbels around the mouth. These sensory organs of touch and taste help the fish to find suitable food in the darkness of the deep.

One of the cod group, the ling can be heavier than the cod itself. This one weighed 26kg(57lb 5oz), but larger ones have been caught at over 30kg(66lb) and in the past they were known to reach weights of over 55kg(121lb). The predatory ling is the heaviest member of the commercially valuable cod family, but it has been so extensively trawled that its future is in doubt.

The cod's coloration reflects the area where it feeds. It was once thought that cod of different colours were separate species. Huge shoals of cod used to swarm through the English Channel, eating their way through mussel-beds and vast numbers of crabs, but this fish is now under threat.

With a mouth even larger than that of the cod, the pollack circles around the rigging of wrecks, feeding on the small fish that hunt for food among the weed growth.

❏ The young of the haddock on both sides of the North Atlantic often shelter among swarms of jellyfishes to avoid the attentions of predators

❏ A ling measuring 1.5m(5ft) was found to be carrying over 28 million eggs - a record among any vertebrate animal.

❏ Perhaps the strangest member of the cod family is the burbot, found in the fresh waters of Europe, Asia and North America. It does not look like its saltwater relatives, being eel-like and only active when the light is poor. The female is known to carry some 3 million eggs, but in spite of its apparently high fertility, the burbot is now becoming rare due to the effects of pollution.

❏ The blue whiting, also known as the poutassou, is an open ocean codfish of the eastern North Atlantic, Iceland, Barents Sea, Mediterranean and Adriatic. It forms huge shoals from the surface down to over 372m(1,200 ft). As with many vividly coloured fish, its blue back fades quickly after death. Some fishing authorities feel that blue whiting could take the place of cod as an important commercial food fish - until overfishing also brings it to the point of extinction!

❏ Heaps of cod bones in Mesolithic deposits (about 12,000 years old) are clear evidence that the fish formed an everyday part of the diet of many prehistoric peoples.

The amazing sea dragons, seahorses and pipefishes

Sea dragons are not huge, fire-breathing fishy monsters, although they do have the mythical dragon's long bony snout and look distinctly weird - rather like seahorses festooned with tendrils of seaweed. In fact, the body of the leafy sea dragon found off southern Australia sprouts appendages that mimic the seaweed in which it lives. The sea dragons are related to the seahorses and pipefishes; all have armoured bodies and swim slowly about, propelled by small fluttering fins. Their armour is composed of rigid rings that cover the body and give these fishes a segmented look. The stately seahorses use their prehensile tails to anchor themselves to seaweeds and coral branches. When they reproduce, the female uses a tube to place the eggs inside a pouch on the male's abdomen. Here, the eggs are fertilized and stay for up to two months while they develop into miniature seahorses. Pipefishes look fairly snakelike and the 60cm(24in)-long snake pipefish looks even more like a snake than a fish as it lurks among the fronds of eel-grass. Practically nothing is known about the breeding habits of this Atlantic species, with few ever coming up in deep-trawl nets. A Florida pipefish exhibits a sensuous mating display, the sexes entwining gracefully while swimming upright.

The dorsal fin and tiny pectoral fins are the seahorse's sole means of propulsion in the water.

The long snout is typical of the European species of seahorse and the shape of the head is remarkably like that of a horse. The segmented body is encased in bands of rigid armour.

Among the seaweeds of the Australian shallows, the leafy sea dragon, *Phycodurus eques*, is almost invisible and protected from potential predators.

This remarkable 'living vegetation' is not just attached to, but actually growing from, the fish. Inside it, there is a slender pipefish.

This sea dragon, also known as the ghost pipefish, lives in the Red Sea.

The extraordinary growths on the sea dragon make it impossible to know which way the fish is pointing, thus confusing predators that seize prey by the head.

❑ Of the 30 or so seahorses, the smallest is only 4cm(1.6in) long. Perhaps we should call it a sea pony?

❑ The deep dragonfish is found at depths of 2,300m (just over 7,500ft) in the seas around Antarctica.

❑ The blue-striped pipefish of the Indo-Pacific can mature at only 2.5cm(1in) and its squat shape makes it more of a sausage-fish than a pipefish!

❑ With their long, tubelike mouths, feeding could be a problem for seahorses and pipefishes. They feed on small crustaceans by using the elongated mouth as a siphon, probing crevices and clumps of weed and then simply sucking in the food items.

Just visible among the 'leaves' is the sea dragon's eye. Even its snout bears small living branches.

Lying head-up in the eel-grass, this pipefish has secured an excellent hiding place. Similar 'camouflaging' behaviour is also seen among other slender-bodied fishes.

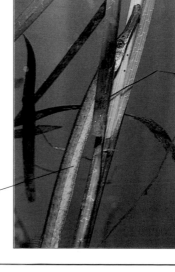

❑ The 'armoured' plates and rings found on seahorses and pipefishes, shown clearly in the above X-ray, are made of osseine, a proteinaceous substance composed of calcium, phosphorus, sulphur and amino acids.

Coral fishes – dazzling to deceive their enemies

The copper-band butterflyfish is common on tropical reefs. As the fish browses, it uses its long snout to pick off food items in the rocky crevices.

The dazzle-painted camouflage of warships in World War Two was designed to break up their outline and confuse the enemy about their size and course. The fishes that live among the brilliantly coloured corals of tropical seas have evolved their own dazzle paint for the same purpose - to foil predators. Coral fishes have splotches and patches of incredible colour, false eye-spots or eyes disguised by coloured patterns - all intended to confuse would-be attackers and make them nearly invisible in their natural habitat. Black bars or bands across the body or even down the eyes of a fish are another effective form of breaking up the shape of the body or making it appear quite different. Hovering amid weed and coral branches, the sergeant major fish, with its silvery body overlaid with five vertical dark bars, is virtually invisible. A newly discovered toadfish found in shallow Mexican seas has a long body with light blue spots on a dark background, while the head is striped in the same colours, giving the appearance of a fish half its size. Many species of butterflyfishes and angelfishes have vivid disruptive markings in spectacular whites, yellows, blues and reds. Out of their environment in a bare aquarium these vivid markings appear garish and unnatural, but in the crevices and holes of the coral reef these thin, deep-bodied fishes are almost impossible to see. The mandarinfish, splendidly confusing in its blotchy blue-green and vivid yellow livery, has added a nasty smell to further confuse and deter predators in the brightly lit waters.

This adult emperor angelfish has a dark bar hiding the eye. The juvenile is even gaudier.

The clown, or big-spotted, triggerfish has highly distinctive markings. The eye is disguised in a dark blotch while the belly is festooned with large white spots that effectively break up the fish's outline in its coral habitat.

The eyes of the copper-band butterflyfish are camouflaged by a stripe that runs down the fish's body, breaking up its outline to confuse predators.

The copper-band butterflyfish has a colourful false eye-spot just in front of the tailfin, suggesting that its head is at the end where this big 'eye' is. When threatened by a would-be predator aiming for the false eye, the fish simply flicks its tail and makes its escape.

❏ The triggerfish above shows an excellent example of dazzle camouflage. The white-edged yellow part of the head looks exactly like a pair of large, open jaws. The real mouth is much smaller.

❏ The juveniles of many coral fishes are quite differently patterned compared to the adults. The young twin-spot wrasse, for example, has two bright, 'attention-diverting' orange spots on the back half of its white body whereas its eyes are 'lost' in a rash of black spots that cover its head - all highly confusing to the hungry predator's steely eye. The adult has a more sedate colour scheme of green with yellow-edged purple fins.

❏ In one species of angelfish the disruptive 'scribbles' on the tailfin are said to resemble Arabic script depicting phrases from the Koran. These markings occur as the juveniles mature into adults. Not surprisingly, the aptly named Koran angelfish is revered by Arabic fishermen and commands a relatively high price.

Camouflage – the subtle art of concealment

Most fish that spend their time on or close to the seabed or riverbed are able to adapt their coloration and have body shapes that help them blend in with their surroundings. The skates and rays are prime examples of this technique of concealment. Among the flatfishes, the plaice is remarkable in its ability to match the colour and texture of the seabed; over a background of small pale pebbles the usual red spots become muted to complete the camouflage. Many midwater fishes can also change colour rapidly to match their backgrounds. The Nassau grouper, for example, can put on quite a colour show as brown to blue stripes and bands quickly appear and disappear on its substantial body, effectively concealing it from intended prey among a rapidly changing vista of coral outgrowths and sandy clearings. Camouflage can also involve behaviour. Mimicking plant stems and leaves is a favourite ploy among fishes. Juvenile batfishes avoid predation by flipping over on their sides and 'playing dead' like mangrove leaves suspended in the water. Fishes called tripletails also mimic mangrove leaves, but the South American leaf-fish uses its leaflike shape, colour and behaviour not only to avoid attack but also to surprise unwitting prey and literally suck them into its protrusible mouth. The thin body of the needlefish looks very much like the stem of a water plant, and gar pikes often hang motionless at the surface like floating twigs and branches. The plant lookalike technique is also employed by black spadefishes in subtropical areas of the Atlantic Ocean. These fishes, measuring up to 90cm(36in) long and 9kg(20lb) in weight, lie on their sides on or close to the bottom, where they look exactly like plant debris. This fools the prey-fish that approach to investigate a possible meal and end up becoming one.

Tendrils and flaps of loose skin disguise the sargassofish as it lurks among the weeds in the Sargasso Sea.

The leaf-fish is invisible among the dead brown leaves drifting in the waters of the Amazon. When the leaves are green, the fish changes colour to match.

Like its close relative the brill, and many other fishes, the turbot has pigment cells in its skin that change its colour patterns to match the seabed on which it is resting. Effective camouflage is the best strategy for fishes that would otherwise be 'sitting targets' for any predators on the lookout for food.

It is easy to see how unwitting creatures become the prey of this superbly camouflaged scorpionfish.

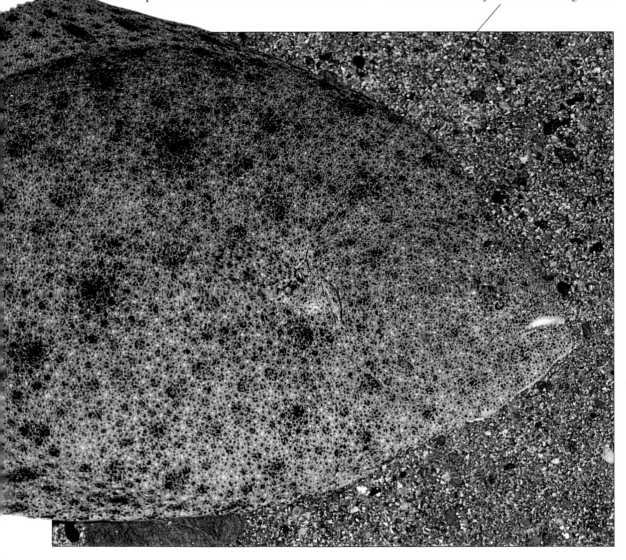

The blotched and tattered pectoral fin of the scorpionfish blurs its outline in the water.

The spotted top surface of the turbot matches the sandy-coloured background.

❏ Exactly how do fishes change colour? Pigments - black, red, orange or yellow - in the skin are contained in branching cells called chromatophores that are richly supplied with nerve fibers. Each colour has its own set of chromatophores. It seems that nerve impulses cause the pigment to move out of the branches of the chromatophores, making the skin go pale, while chemicals produced by the brain have the reverse effect of causing the pigment to spread out along the branches of the chromatophores and make the skin appear darker. The main stimulus for colour change comes via the eyes, with a layer behind the retina controlling the release of colour-changing hormone.

❏ A plaice in a tank with a black-and-white checkered base can almost produce this pattern on its body.

❏ The yellow-spotted ray (above) from the Caribbean can blend so well with the sand that it is practically invisible to the casual eye.

Fishes with stars in their eyes

Fishes' eyes have developed in a number of ways. The stargazers, for example, have eyes on top of their heads and can only look upwards. These fish bury themselves in the sand, with their eyes ideally positioned to locate likely fish as prey and also to spot predators. A number of stargazer species live off the Pacific coast of North America, in the Indian Ocean and Australian waters at depths down to 272m(780ft). All have the same lifestyle and one, the 30cm(12in) European stargazer, is able to give off electric pulses that alert the fish to prey creeping towards it over the seabed. The electric organs of this fish are believed to be modified eye muscles. It lies buried in the sand, its mouth fringed with quivering flaps to entice food-fish. The eyes of the 10cm(4in) sand stargazer from the West Indies are set on small stalks and probably perceive the same view as 'fish-eye' camera lenses. Upward-looking eyes are not confined to the bottom-living stargazers. One freshwater fish, with the apt common name of 'four-eyes', has eyes divided into two halves for seeing both above and beneath the water surface. In the coastal and muddy fresh waters of Central and South America in which it lives, this bifocal arrangement allows the fish to find the insects on and above the surface as well as to keep a lookout for predators approaching from below.

The European stargazer, with its large head and sharply tapering body, typical of these fishes. It is common in the Mediterranean Sea, but is also found off the Atlantic coast of Spain and Portugal.

Only the upward-staring eyes and the fringed mouth of the electric stargazer are visible as it lies buried in the sandy seabed.

The eyes of the aptly named four-eyed fish are divided, so that it can see above and below the water.

The four-eyed fish lives in the estuarine waters of Central and South America. It produces up to five live young at a time.

A stalked flap of skin below the lip twitches to attract fish fry close enough to be snapped up.

FACT FILE

❏ The flatfishes, skates and rays have eyes that can only stare upwards, but some have eyes that can rotate like periscopes to give them a panoramic view. Strangest of all eye positions is that of the aptly named hammerhead shark. On either side of its head are wing-shaped projections with eyes at the tip.

❏ Most stargazers are armed with poisonous dorsal spines for defence and killing prey. They also have the ability to produce electric shocks, lethal to other fishes and even painful to the hand.

❏ This underwater view of the four-eyed fish, *Anableps anableps*, shows that the top half of the eye is held above the water surface. Each eye is divided into two parts by a bridge of tissue that cuts across the cornea, pupil and retina. The view from above is focused on the bottom part of the retina, while images of objects below the fish are focused on the top part of the retina. In effect, this fish has a very sophisticated version of bifocal lenses! In its shallow water habitat, this system gives it all-round awareness.

Shining lights of the fish world

The pine-cone fish has these light-emitting pits below the jaws, 'powered' by bacteria.

Sunlight cannot penetrate to the ocean depths, and darkness reigns below 186m(600ft), even in the clearest waters. Beyond that there is total blackness, water pressure increases and it is very cold – with temperatures as low as $3^0C(37.7^0F)$. Nevertheless, there is life in this seemingly inhospitable environment, including strange light-bearing fishes that are sometimes transparent, often grotesque. The value of these lights is uncertain, because most of the fishes that live down in the blackness of the depths are blind! It is possible that light attracts prey fish, but there is a danger that it also advertises the presence of one predator to another. Light patterns vary among fishes and may well be a recognition signal for mates. The light produced by fishes comes from two sources; certain fishes have colonies of luminous bacteria located in areas below the skin, and some species are able to lower 'shutters' to control the light. This is the same 'living' light that makes the firefly and the glowworm (the wingless larva of the firefly) shine in the dark. The so-called bioluminescence is created when a substance called luciferin is oxidized in the presence of an enzyme called luciferase. The light is simply a form of energy released by the chemical reaction, and is almost like photosynthesis in reverse. The other kind of light produced by fishes shines from modified mucous glands called photophores that can be switched on and off by the nervous system. The skin of some fishes also becomes luminous at times from numbers of slime-containing pores.

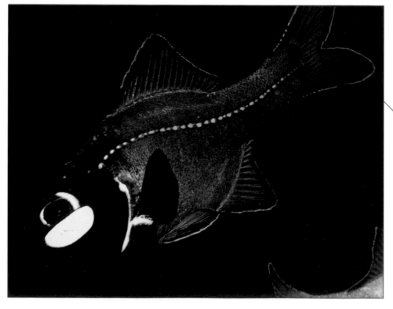

The rounded sacs below the eyes of this flashlight fish glow white in the dark. The fish can turn them on and off and uses them to attract the planktonic animals that becomes its prey

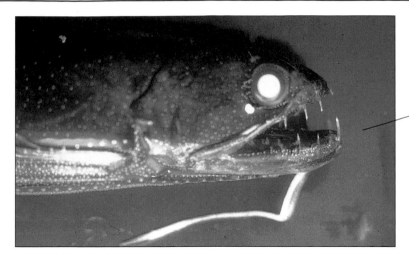

Taken in ultraviolet light, this photograph of the black star eater highlights the luminous organs festooning the fish. At 1,000m (3,300ft) these lights put on quite a show!

Sloane's viperfish, up to 30cm(12in) long, even has lights inside the mouth and glowing spots near the eyes to illuminate possible food.

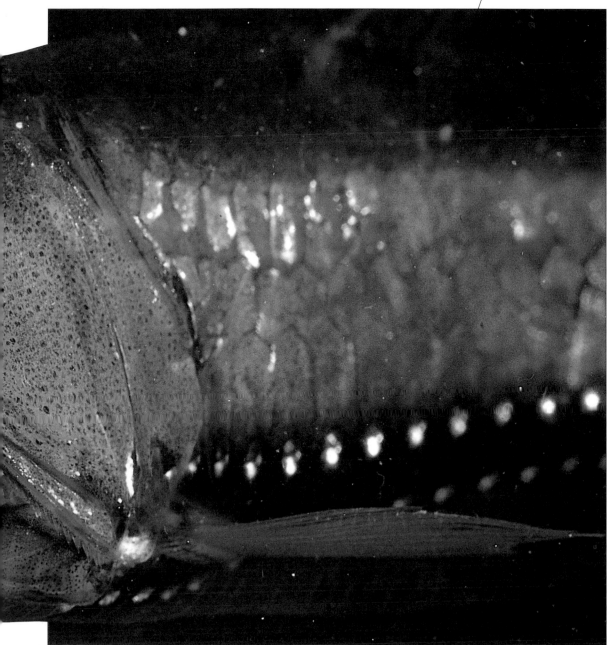

FACT FILE

❑ Not all luminous fishes live in the depths of the sea; one 10cm(4in) lanternfish from the waters of the North Atlantic and Mediterranean can be seen in large numbers, with bright patterns of blue lights gleaming near the tail.

❑ The 38cm(15in) plainfin midshipman has some 700 white-light photophores along its body, which can flash as the fish is held in the hands. It is called the midshipman because it can make a sound like a naval pipe.

❑ The deepsea lanternfish, shown above, lives at depths of 400-614m(1,310-2,000ft). The photophores on the underside break up its outline when viewed from below.

❑ There are two small related light-emitting fishes in the Indian Ocean. They have bar-shaped pits beneath the eyes that hold symbiotic bacteria that glow when supplied with oxygen. Fishermen remove these organs and put them on their hooks to attract fish.

❑ Biologists can use patterns of light organs to distinguish between species of fish.

Fishes with wandering eyes

It is one of the strangest events in all animal life: when a flatfish is hatched, it is a normal, tiny 'round' fish. The embryo, with its attached yolk-sac, has eyes in the usual place, on either side of the head. It swims normally on the surface or in midwater, searching for minute food particles. But after a few weeks, the body beings to deepen and one eye starts on a strange migration around the head towards the other eye. At the same time, the fish sinks to the seabed, where it spends the rest of its life lying on one side. This 'bottom' surface remains a dull grey-white, while the 'top' side – now with two eyes – usually develops a brown or spotted pattern that can be adapted so that it matches the colour and texture of the seabed on which it is lying. Some flatfishes never develop a coloured 'top' surface; instead they remain white, although there usually is a small patch of colour on the head. For some unknown reason there is a delay in the eye migration of some flatfishes. The dorsal fin forms along what was the back (now the side) of the fish, with the result that instead of 'sliding round the head' the eye has to move through the tissue between the fin and the bone of the cranium, eventually closing on the other eye. It is not uncommon for the 'wrong' eye to migrate and when this occurs the fish becomes a mirror image of its species, with both eyes on the 'wrong' side. There are 'righthanded' and 'lefthanded' flatfishes. The flounder, plaice, dab, halibut, witch and sole have eyes on the original right side, while the turbot, megrim and brill have their eyes on the left side of the body.

Some flatfishes, such as this turbot, have fringes around the mouth. The eyes are close together, which is typical of the sole family of fishes.

Eyes on stalks enable flatfishes to see, even if they are buried in sand.

❏ While one eye in a juvenile flatfish migrates over the cranium to join the other, the gill covers of the flatfishes remain on both sides of the fish. Because these fishes spend their adult lives on one side, a channel has developed between the gill cavities so that when the flatfish 'breathes out' all the water is expelled from the upper gill cover.

❏ There are some 600 flatfish species, widespread from the Arctic to the tropics and from shallow inshore waters to depths of 1,830m(6,000ft).

❏ Most flatfishes weigh no more than 0.5-1kg(1.1-2.2lb), but the Atlantic halibut can reach a weight of 317kg(700lb) and grow 2.4m(8ft) long.

❏ The name 'halibut' is derived from the name 'holy fish' because it was traditionally eaten on holy days.

❏ Fossil flatfishes have been found in rock deposits up to 16 million years old.

In this winter flounder, both eyes have become bulbous, giving some forward vision.

The flounder's eyes move independently, so the fish has all-round vision.

The mouth slants towards the top side of the adult.

This colourful flounder from the Virgin Isles has a distinctive notch in front of one eye, marking the path of the eye's migration.

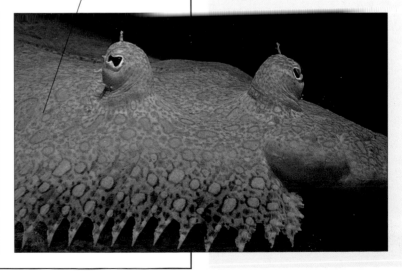

Freshwater piranha and marine bluefish

In the waters of the Lower Amazon, the freshwater piranha has a notorious reputation – and in this case it is well deserved. Measuring about 60cm(24in) long, the biggest piranha swim in shoals searching for food – any food so long as it is animal, dead or alive. A shoal of piranhas will reduce a 45kg(100lb) animal to a skeleton in a minute, the razorlike teeth slicing quickly through flesh. One report tells of a rider and his horse being eaten while attempting to cross a river inhabited by piranha. Only bones and the man's clothes remained. The bite of a piranha resembles that of a shark; it lunges at and wrestles with a hunk of meat and having cut it free, gulps it down. Not only is the dentition of the piranha formidable, but the fish swarm onto a food source in such numbers that there is no escape. There are about 25 species of piranha, but only one fifth of these are savage enough to threaten a wounded animal in the water. Most feed on fish and similar prey. The 1.8m(6ft) marine bluefish found in tropical coastal waters is just as ferocious. It hunts in huge shoals and will attack more fish than it can eat.

The piranhas well-muscled body is ideal for lungeing towards its prey and hanging onto its struggling victim.

Unlike most fish teeth, those of the piranha are set in sockets and not simply embedded in the jaw.

The business end of the notorious piranha, showing the interlocking cutting teeth. Once closed over the prey item, the piranha wriggles like a shark until the mouthful is torn away.

❏ It is said that piranhas retain active enough muscular activity when dead to snap at the hand picking them up.

At a telltale sign of blood in the water, this shoal of piranha will swim at high speed towards the source of their next meal, led on by their keen sense of smell and taste.

❏ Shoals of bluefish, as shown above, consist of fish of the same size. Packs of hunting bluefish will even turn on themselves in a feeding frenzy, and smaller individuals just do not last long enough to be accepted in the shoal.

❏ The razor-sharp teeth of piranhas are used by Orinoco Indians to tip their arrows.

❏ Young bluefish are known as snappers, presumably because of their inclination to snap at anything in sight.

❏ Piranha home-in on their food in the same way as sharks, by following the smell of blood or flesh in the water.

❏ Like the well-known New York sewer crocodile scare, piranha have been reported as being released into US public waters by aquarists tired of feeding them. This led to a ban on their importation

Unwary fishermen have lost a finger to the jaws of a piranha, even in its death throes.

Wash-and-brush-up fishes

Hovering over coral reefs, where shafts of bright sunlight pierce the crystal waters and make the underwater world shimmer in a dance of moving patterns, large fishes often queue up for the attentions of small fishes that scurry and bustle around them, nibbling at loose skin, flaky scales or parasites. Patiently, large groupers hold their capacious mouths open, while little fish swim inside, cleaning the sharp teeth! Even the very sensitive gills are given the cleaner's attention. There are more than 24 species of marine cleanerfish, all working in perfect safety, even from usually very aggressive predators. One of these is the slender blue-streak cleaner wrasse from the Indian and Pacific Oceans. It cheekily waits for customers at its recognized 'cleaning stations' on the reef. Even large predatory fishes will join the queue, taking their turn for the blue streak wrasse to peck and nibble at parasites on the body. It might be easy to attribute a human 'caring' attitude to the acts of the cleanerfishes but, like human life, all is not as innocent as it seems. Nature has also thought of the sneaky disguise and there are fishes that look like cleaners and take advantage of larger fishes that come up for a 'going over'. Typical of these counterfeit cleanerfishes is a small but well-toothed blenny, the aptly named false cleanerfish. It is not interested in parasites or dead skin, but contents itself by taking bites of living tissue out of any unsuspecting 'clients' that come close, mistaking it for a harmless 'real' cleanerfish.

Its cavernous jaws agape, this Australian blue grouper is having the inside of its mouth cleaned by an industrious blue streak cleanerfish. Parasites, fungus and pieces of dead skin all provide a meal for the cleanerfish.

This 'client' fish may have waited in line for the cleaning services it needs.

This diminutive cleaner is a small blenny that resembles the blue streak. It is cleaning a large red-banded grouper that could easily devour it.

❏ The 'loud' coloration of the cleanerfishes, usually in the form of a blue stripe along the body, may well be a form of advertising, for they are easily seen against their background. Most fishes would flee from known predators, but the cleanerfishes wear a 'cloak of immunity' and wait patiently as they are approached.

❏ The cleanerfishes found in the tropical West Atlantic and those in the Indo-Pacific are two different groups separated by vast distances of ocean, yet they both share the same distinctive blue 'cleaner' stripe along the side of the body.

❏ Some cleanerfishes have become 'living tweezers', with teeth adapted to pulling at the loose scales and parasites of their customers.

❏ One of the many gobies is a cleanerfish measuring only 4cm(1.6in) long. Named the shark-nosed goby because of its curved, underslung mouth, this tiny Caribbean fish hovers in position over a certain coral peak waiting for the arrival of 'customers' needing attention.

❏ Remoras (pages 38-39) also acts as cleanerfish, using their suction discs to advantage when seeking out parasites.

❏ Some shrimps have become cleaners to fishes. They also have bright body patterns to attract attention and twitch their antennae as a signal for 'client' fishes to approach.

The blue streak wrasse, found in the Indo-Pacific, prefers to pick parasites off fish rather than scavenge for bits of food dropped by its 'customers'. A number of its 'clients' are normally predatory, but adopt a passive attitude when being cleaned.

A wimplefish allows a blue streak cleanerfish, *Labroides dimidiatus*, to give it a thorough clean. The wimplefish will have come to the cleanerfish's territory, which it defends against the entry of any potential rivals.

Pet fishes – companions in the home

The wild form of the platy was discovered in Central America in 1866. In comparison to the ornamental forms, the wild fish is drab and unspectacular.

For hundreds or perhaps even thousands of years, people have kept fish indoors in glass containers. One problem with petfishes is their potential size. While young, a tench, carp or roach will thrive in a well-kept indoor aquarium. But 'well-kept' means well-fed, and these fishes can soon outgrow the modest fish tank. Outdoor ponds can provide good homes for many fish species, but beware perch or small pike, for these predators will help themselves to other resident fish. Waterbirds, herons and the next-door 'friendly' cat will also take advantage of an alfresco meal! Tropical aquarium fishes need suitable warmth and sufficient oxygenation to thrive. Small catfishes are often kept for their scavenging action on the tank gravel, thus helping to keep the water clean. Typical small and colourful aquarium fishes include swordtails and guppies. Many such fishes are livebearers and fishkeeping becomes even more interesting when clouds of tiny fry appear, although overstocking the tank can be counter productive. Marine fishes can also be kept in home aquariums but, although modern technology offers help in the shape of 'artificial' sea salts and complex life-support systems, the problems of maintaining a stable environment make this quite a challenge.

Goldfish make attractive pets in a well-maintained and tastefully decorated aquarium.

Platies, from
Central America,
are toothcarps with
well-developed but
small teeth in their jaws.

Platies are all livebearers.
The male transfers his
sperm to the female by
means of modified anal
fin rays. Following a
single transfer, the
female can produce
several generations of
live young.

Note the spine at the
base of the gill-cover of
this angelfish. It
differentiates it from the
otherwise identical
butterflyfishes. Like other colourful
reef fishes, angelfishes provide exotic
interest in a marine aquarium.

Aquarists have
developed many highly
coloured varieties of the
platy, such as these
attractive golden sunset
wagtail platies.

❑ Some petfishes are sent around the world as fertilized eggs and all the aquarist has to do is add water for almost instant fish. These fishes are called egglaying toothcarps that normally live in temporary ponds in the tropics. During the dry season, all that remains of the previous generation of fishes are their fertilized eggs lying dormant in the bottom sediment. When the rains return, the eggs hatch and the fry grow rapidly, reach sexual maturity and spawn a new batch of fertilized eggs before they die - all in the space of one year. Biologists are particularly interested in these fishes because they include mosquito larvae as part of their diet. In countries where the malaria-carrying mosquito abounds, it has been possible literally to 'seed' stretches of stagnant water with these fish eggs to produce shoals of natural predators of the mosquito larvae. To help speed up the good work, biologists have been able to reduce the hatching time of the eggs to a matter of a few minutes.

❑ The Romans and, before them, the Chinese built large outdoor ponds in which they kept colourful fish both for food and entertaining guests.

❑ The world's first large public aquarium, exhibiting a wide range of exotic fishes, was constructed in the Regent's Park Zoo in London and was opened in 1853.

The grunting gurnards

The armour-plated skull is clearly visible in this gurnard, *Trigla lucerna*, and there are spines protruding from the gill-covers.

The gurnards are colourful marine fishes, strangely armoured on the head and equipped with long fin rays with which they can 'walk' on the seabed. The thick plates covering the head give the fishes a cowlike appearance when viewed from certain angles, and the sides of the body are also armoured with stout plates, called scutes. The pectoral fins are large and the fingerlike extensions are covered with sensory organs that help the fish to 'feel' the seabed when walking with the fins extended. Gurnards are found throughout the world and were once widely known as 'sea robins', perhaps because of the deep red body colour of some species. A particularly colourful species is the 32cm(12.5in) flying gurnard found in the Atlantic Ocean from Massachusetts south to Argentina in the west and to the Iberian Peninsula, Mediterranean and West Africa in the east. It has huge pectoral fins with bright blue spots on a red background, sometimes the sign of a predatory or poisonous animal, but this gurnard is harmless. Gurnards are able to make very audible grunting noises by contracting their muscles around the swimbladder, which acts like a sounding board to amplify the vibrations. This is unlikely to be a form of communication, however, other than to signal their presence among their own kind.

The gurnards show great variations in body colour depending on the seabed where they live. Like most fishes, this grey gurnard can adapt its coloration to match its surroundings.

The flying gurnard's huge pectoral fins are used both for 'flying' through the water and for brief glides above the surface, as well as to deter predators by making the fish appear much larger than it really is.

Note the 'leading edge flaps' on the flying gurnard, one of Nature's more advanced aerodynamic experiments.

❑ Most gurnards have gill covers armed with sharp spines that can make handling these fish a painful business.

❑ One rare species, the armoured sea robin, has strange feathery tentacles sprouting from its chin.

Were the gurnards much larger, they would look formidable! These fishes can rest quite well on the seabed, supported by the thickened and strengthened rays of the pectoral fins.

The grunts are not produced by the mouth, but by muscles contracting around the swimbladder.

❑ The long rays of the pectoral spines, as clearly shown on the tub gurnard above, are so sensitive that they almost certainly include taste organs as well as touch receptors.

❑ Going white with fear is not only a human trait, the red gurnard's colour has been known to turn white when it is disturbed or alarmed.

❑ The flying gurnard is not only able to make short glides through the air, it can also walk on its long pelvic fins, which move one at a time like 'conventional' legs.

The versatile carp family

The crucian carp never grows to the bulky size of the common carp.

The common carp, one of a very large family of freshwater fishes, has many relatives throughout the world, except in Australia, New Zealand, South America and Madagascar. Man has introduced the common carp into many countries without an indigenous carp population, sometimes with unfortunate consequences. In the USA, for example, the introduced carp has become a nuisance in many waters, where it has bred prolifically to the detriment of the native fish species. The mirror carp, with its few large scales, and the leather carp, with its smooth, scaleless body, are variants of the common carp. These powerful fish can all grow to a weight in excess of 13.6kg(30lb). The crucian carp is smaller, as is its relative, the goldfish. It was random colour changes in common carp that led to the development of koi, a type of ornamental carp that can trace its origins back to black common carp from eastern Asia and China over 2,000 years ago. The vast range of colour types seen today - most famously bred by the Japanese - have been cultivated and 'fine-tuned' from red, white and yellow mutations noticed by rice farmers in an isolated province of Japan in the early 1800s. Today, koi keeping enjoys a fanatical following in many countries around the world and superb examples of these fish command high prices among dedicated enthusiasts.

Breeding koi, the most colourful variety of carp, has become a specialist trade.

In the mirror carp, pictured here, the scales are few and large, while the leather carp is scaleless. King varieties of this freshwater fish can reach a weight of 32kg(70lb). Fossil carp are known from 10 million years ago.

There are over 100 colour varieties of koi, each with Japanese names that describe such features as the basic colour, the bold markings, the arrangement of the scales and their lustre, as well as references to periods of Japanese history.

❑ The Chinese grass carp can weigh up to 32kg(70lb) and has its uses in weed-control. Where conditions are warm enough and the flow is right, this fish will clear the area of weeds and breed. It also makes a fine food fish.

❑ Few fish would fetch £150,000, but one 91cm(32in)-long, red-and-white koi did sell for that sum. Breeding koi has become very big business in Japan, Europe and the USA.

❑ A 3m(10ft)-long carp from Thailand is caught on hooks baited with balls of rice. This carp, a noted food fish, is so strong it has been known to pull fishing boats along!

❑ A North American carp, known as the Colorado squawfish, can weigh 36kg(80lb) and reach 1.5m(5ft) long. The Indians used it as a food fish and white men, thinking it a game fish, called it the white salmon.

❑ It is said that when the French Queen Antoinette was guillotined during the French Revolution her pet carp suffered the same fate.

❑ In 1952, the largest carp caught in the UK, and named 'Clarissa', was kept in London Zoo and fed on dog biscuits until she died in 1972. She weighed 19.8kg(44lb), but was later superseded by one weighing 23kg(51lb). However, in 1986, a carp from Italy was found to weigh 32kg(70.5lb).

Fishes with flights of fancy

The flying gurnard spreads its blue-spotted pectoral fins as a warning to predators, and can make brief 'skips' out of the water.

One fish can really fly. This is the common hatchetfish, a 6cm(2.4in) freshwater species found in the waters of the Amazon River and in Guyana. Its 'wings' - the pectoral fins - move so fast that this small fish leaves the water and flies along just above the surface, making a buzzing sound as it goes. Strangely, the well-known marine flying fishes can only glide. These so-called 'flying' fishes spread their large pectoral fins and leap clear of the surface to glide through the air, while the related 'halfbeaks' can only skitter across the surface on their tailfins without rising above it. Unless it is affected by the wind, the glide is always in a straight line, proving that these fish have no flying control. At the end of the glide, the ventral fins act as airbrakes, slowing the fish down as it enters the water headfirst. Before breaking the surface, flying fish swim at high speeds - up to 56kph(35mph) - to reach 'take-off' velocity. The 'flights' - measuring as much as 335m(1,100ft) - have been attributed to exuberance, but are more likely to be a means of escape from predatory fishes, such as the sailfish or marlin. To the surprise of sailors, marine flying fish often land on the decks of boats! Because these fishes are surface-feeders their eyes are positioned so that they have downward vision, which may also help them to evade predators.

Powerful muscles control the tailfin and provide the initial propulsion that enables all flying fishes to build up sufficient speed in the water before launching briefly above the surface.

Although the pectoral fins are the main means of flight, all the fins come into use, including the long anal fin running along the keel. The flat dorsal surface of the fish and the deep belly create an ideal streamlined shape.

The long pectoral fins of this silver hatchetfish are its means of flight, but it can only make short aerial trips.

The deep body of the silver hatchetfish is typical of the characin group to which they belong. As these freshwater fishes of the Amazon area of South America scuttle across the surface, they strike the water with their long pectoral fins just before lifting off, but their 'flight' is only a short one.

Four-winged flying fish photographed in the Red Sea. It is not unknown for flying fishes accidentally to land on a vessel's deck. The reason is that once airborne, the fishes have no control of their flight-path and fall out of the air in the same way that a paper dart, once launched, will continue until it floats to the ground.

Having worked up sufficient speed under water with the tailfin, flying fishes break through the surface and their extended pectoral wings supply enough 'lift' for them to remain airborne.

❑ The freshwater butterflyfish (shown above) lives in quiet waters in Africa and can leap above the surface to catch flying insects. It does not flap its large pectoral fins like the hatchetfishes, but uses them as simple gliding aerofoils. These fish are only 10cm(4in) long and can be kept in an aquarium, but it is essential to cover the top securely to prevent them 'flying' out!

❑ The ventral,or pelvic, fins of the Atlantic flying fish also extend at the same time as the larger pectoral fins, and in 'flight' the fish resembles a biplane! Presumably these two wings give the fish more stability in the air, but it is not able to steer very effectively.

❑ Marine flying fishes are creatures of the open ocean and lay large eggs with sticky filaments that cling to clumps of floating seaweed.

❑ The freshwater balao, or ballyhoo, is one of the largest flying fishes, reaching 45cm(18in) in length. As well as being able to glide through the air on its pectoral fins, the ballyhoo can also 'stand' for long periods on the riverbed, using its finrays as supports.

Foul poison and deadly venom

About 45 species of bony and cartilaginous fishes have poison-filled spines or gill-covers for offence or defence and are capable of inflicting serious wounds. Most poisonous fishes live in warm tropical waters. These include the beautiful but deadly turkeyfishes, scorpionfishes and lionfishes found in the Red Sea and in the Indian and Pacific Oceans. They carry long venomous spines on the extended rays of the dorsal and pectoral fins. Even in colder Northern European waters a similar danger lurks in the form of weever fishes that lie buried in sand close inshore and reward an unwary foot with an injection of painful poison. The sands of tropical beaches of India and Australia hold a similarly unwelcome surprise for careless bathers in the shape of the stonefish, which can cause an agonisingly painful wound, with numbness spreading through the body and the chance that limbs may become gangrenous and require amputation. Stingrays also have notoriously venomous spines on their long, thin tails and their poison can be fatal. It is vital that any wound caused by a venomous spine should be seen by a doctor as soon as possible. Some fish have poisonous mucus, flesh and/or organs, which keep predators at bay and also cause problems if eaten by humans. The flesh of the pufferfish, known as fugu in Japan, can be eaten but its entrails are highly poisonous.

The subtle red and brown coloration of the scorpionfish, also called the turkeyfish, enables it to blend into its habitat of coral reefs. It is found throughout the Indian and Pacific Oceans.

The dorsal and pectoral fins of this 'sea scorpion' are highly venomous and potentially lethal to humans.

The eyes of the stonefish mimic individual corals growing on a tropical reef.

Looking exactly like the rough surface of a coral reef, the stonefish is a serious threat to anyone exploring the shallows of Indo-Pacific islands and atolls. Once the venom is injected from the spines, death often follows after a short period of agony.

If the fish is attacked, venom flows through grooves in the spiny rays of the dorsal and pectoral fins.

❏ The black-saddled pufferfish, or striped toby, (shown above) looks innocent enough, but like other members of its family, the flesh and mucus of this fish contain a virulent toxin. Other fish have learned to leave it alone, but any that have still to find out will be persuaded to spit it out when it swells up inside their mouth.

❏ The harmless leatherjacket, a fish about the same size as the tiny but deadly black-saddled pufferfish has adopted the same body colour and pattern as a very effective deterrent against predators.

❏ Because of the weever's poison, the Romans called it *vipera*, which has become corrupted into 'weever'.

❏ Trawlermen who get the weever's poison in their hands have been known to jump overboard because of the very severe pain. Fish poisons can cause delerium and fever, and the weever's sting has resulted in heart failure in some cases

❏ The beautiful blue-spotted stingray found in tropical shallows carries one or two deadly stings in its long tail .

'White death' and other sharks

Immensely powerful, the great white shark can grow to a length of 6.4m(21ft).

About 350 shark species have evolved over a period of 450 million years to become the supreme predators. They are not confined to tropical waters, being found in every sea, and they are known to travel huge distances; a blue shark tagged off New York was recorded near Spain; sharks tagged in UK waters have been seen off Brazil, and one nurse shark was judged to have travelled 320,000km(200,000 miles) in six years of circling its Australian aquarium. Not all sharks will attack man on sight - although many will do so in self-defence - but the great white shark's ferocity is well known. Also called the 'white death', it was probably responsible for most of the 1,200 attacks on humans recorded over nine years in one US Navy survey. A shark's feeding behavior can be alerted by incredibly small quantities of blood in the water and sharks are also attracted by the vibrations created by swimmers. According to the Medical Journal of Australia, the disturbance made by between two and ten swimmers appears to create the most attractive vibrations to sharks; for some reason, fewer or more swimmers do not have the same effect. There have been many attempts to devise the perfect shark repellent using a chemical base. However, the current thinking is that products based on repellent substances secreted by other sea creatures could prove effective.

In all sharks, the bones of the vertebrae run up into the upper lobe of the tailfin.

The distinguishing feature of the very widespread blue shark is the long, wing-shaped pectoral fins. These and the tail provide the mobility necessary for one of the sea's most successful predators.

Most sharks have five gill slits.

The well-named hammerhead shark has the eyes and nostrils at the tips of the projections on the head. These 'headwings' also hold electromagnetic organs used for navigation.

Known as the white pointer or, more dramatically, the white death, this shark is found near coasts in many warm seas. Its scientific name, *Carcharodon carcharias*, means 'jagged teeth'.

❏ One of the strangest shark stories relates how the skipper of an eighteenth century ship threw confidential papers overboard while being pursued, so that when his vessel was boarded no useful documentation could be found. Another vessel then came alongside and reported that a shark had been killed and opened - and the ship's papers were found in its stomach.

❏ When a tatooed arm was found in a tiger shark, caught off Sydney in 1935, it solved a murder mystery. The tattoos identified a missing man and a murder charge was brought.

❏ The beach with most recorded shark attacks is Amanzimtoti, 27km(16.5 miles) south of Durban, South Africa.

❏ On an Australian island called Chasm there are rocks with a vivid blood-red stain. The Aborigines say that a tiger shark called Bangudja attacked a 'dolphin-man' there.

❏ A protective secretion produced by the humble sea cucumber when molested could form the basis of an effective shark repellent. If a shark bites a sea cucumber, it quickly releases it and never attacks one again. Tank tests show that the secretion - called holothurin - could kill a 20kg(44lb) shark at a dilution of one part in 600,000. In the open seas, sharks would detect less than a lethal quantity and move away.

Fishes that sleep through droughts

The African lungfishes and their South American and Australian relatives are aptly described as 'living fossils', descendants of a wide variety of lungishes that existed many millions of years ago. They are so-called because the swimbladder, which acts like a buoyancy bag in most other fishes, is adapted into a 'lung' so that the fish can absorb oxygen into the bloodstream by inhaling air directly at the surface. In fact, in their normal habitat, lungfishes must rise to the surface every half an hour to gulp in a 'lungful' of air, but they also use their reduced gills under water. If they are prevented from rising to the surface for air, lungfishes drown. The Australian lungfish has a one-chambered lung, while the African and South American species each have two chambers. An unusual feature of the lungfish's breathing apparatus is an opening from the nostrils to the inside of the mouth, which allows it to breathe air at the surface without opening its mouth. During periods of drought, the African lungfish burrows down into the mud and excretes a slimy coating that hardens to form a waterproof covering and prevents a lethal loss of moisture; its heart rate slows down and the body enters a state of hibernation. While entombed in this mud case, a small opening remains free and linked to the mouth so that it can breathe air. When the water levels rise again, they resume their ordinary lifestyle.

African lungfishes, which can grow over 1.5m(5ft) long, have platelike teeth that continue to grow at the base as they wear down.

The Australian lungfish can walk on the bottom using its strong pectoral and pelvic fins - a reflection of its long ancestory and its links with the emergence of early amphibians.

The fish uses the tactile organs on its fins to inspect food items.

In times of drought, the African lungfish burrows into mud, excretes a cocoon of water-resistant mucus around itself and breathes through a small hole near the mouth. It can continue to breathe in this torpid state until rains bring water to its river or pool again

All lungfishes share this symmetrical tailfin, which tapers to a point without developing the normal 'fish' shape. This is yet another primitive feature of this fascinating group of ancient fishes.

South American lungfishes have ventral fins that develop long, thin filaments, rich in blood vessels. It is thought that these filaments help to aerate the normally murky water in the vicinity of the fish's eggs.

South American lungfishes retreat into a mud-burrow when the rivers dry up and can survive in this moisture-tight environment, although they do not build a cocoon.

FACT FILE

❏ The existence of closely related lungfishes in South America, Africa and Australia points to their probable evolution at a time when the continents were linked together, and before Continental Drift drew them apart to their present positions. Those early lungfishes were related to that other 'living fossil,' the coelacanth (featured on pages 24-25).

❏ In order to test the ability of African lungfishes to survive their dry incarceration in mud protected by a moisture-tight cocoon, one was brought from its native dried-up swamp to a laboratory thousands of miles away. Four years passed before the caked, apparently lifeless fish was extracted, but when placed in water it soon recovered - thin but well.

❏ It is only the African and South American lungfishes that bury themselves in mud when the water in their rivers dries up, although the South American lungfish does not form a cocoon. The Australian lungfish can survive in small pools of stagnant water during the summer but will die if the water disappears completely.

❏ The African and South American lungfishes obtain 98 percent of their oxygen from the air and they have a four-chambered heart and a blood circulation that begins to resemble the system found in primitive amphibians - a clear sign of evolution in action.

The bizarre catfishes

Repulsive, bewhiskered, nocturnal, predatory – the catfishes are the ugly sisters of the fish world. Perhaps the apparent unpleasantness of these fishes is summed up in the cave catfish that lives in the enclosed waters of a cavern near Grootfontein in South West Africa. This blind fish has feeding habits that hardly bear repeating – it feeds on baboon droppings! Cave-dwelling catfish also live in the USA. In the blackness of the Mammoth Cave in Kentucky, for example, lives a blind catfish with sensory organs on its head to compensate for its loss of sight. The female collects all of its eggs into its gill chamber, perhaps so that it does not lose them in the darkness, where they remain until the young hatch. In the fresh waters of Eastern Europe lurks an ugly monster that dwarfs its numerous American relatives. Hidden during the day, the European wels comes out at night to seize large fish, frogs, rodents and ducks. It needs large prey because it can grow to a length of 3m(almost 10ft) and weigh 200kg(440lb). The catfishes really have developed some weird lifestyles. In the waters of some central African lakes, the upside-down catfish literally swims upside-down, the usual colour pattern of dark top and pale underside being reversed in this fish to help it merge into the background as it feeds on algae beneath water plants.

The upside-down catfish from central Africa, has developed its unusual posture through a life of browsing on algae growing on the undersides of water plant leaves.

The wels is a ponderous, ugly carnivore feeding on anything, including fish and small mammals and has even been known to pull ducklings down below the water surface.

The long barbels of the shovelnose catfish are typical of this South American freshwater group. It prowls for prey at night.

The albino variety of the walking catfish is more widely seen in aquariums than the wild brown form. This powerful fish can breathe air as it literally walks across marshy areas in search of food.

Glue can be made from the bones and swimbladder of the extraordinary European wels.

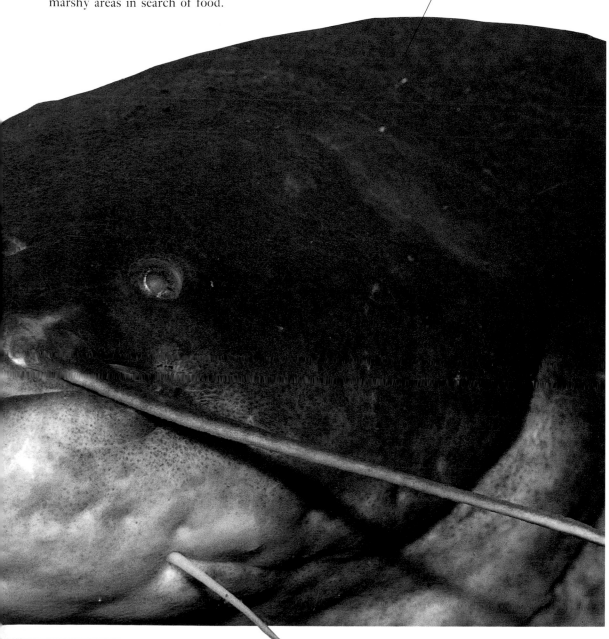

❑ Catfishes received their common name from the whiskery barbels protruding from the corners of their mouths - just like their four-legged counterparts on land.

❑ The largest recorded specimen of the European wels was 5m(16ft 5in) long and weighed 306kg(675lb).

❑ The glass catfish, from Southeast Asia ,shown above, is aptly named for its clear body. The internal organs are near the head end, leaving the rest of the body looking empty. It swims at an angle and is active during daylight hours.

❑ North American fresh waters abound with catfishes bearing evocative names, such as stonecats, flatheads and madtoms - the latter one sporting poisonous spines

❑ The Indian catfish can make sounds by scraping the dorsal fin against its backbone, but even this catfish cannot meow!

❑ Catfishes have a link of tiny bones that transmit vibrations picked up by the swimbladder to the inner ear, effectively boosting their hearing power.

Fishes that blow themselves up

The inexorable process of evolution has resulted in many ways in which fodder animals, those which are subject to predation, can avoid being taken and eaten. For some, speed is the answer, many predators being able to keep up the chase for only a limited period and giving up well before the stamina of their prey is exhausted. Camouflage, too, plays a vital defensive role in the lives of many otherwise defenceless animals. Some species of fish, however, have adopted quite a different strategy to confound any would-be attackers. Several fishes, such as the pufferfishes and porcupinefishes, literally blow themselves up, rapidly taking in water to grotesquely inflate their bodies. Found in marine tropical waters around the world, many of these fishes also have poisonous flesh and are covered with vicious-looking spines. When the body is inflated, these spines serve as a double insurance policy against being swallowed by hungry predators. Unfortunately, their readiness to inflate can be their downfall. When handled, these fishes will inflate themselves and will then float, often upside-down, on the surface at the mercy of wind and waves. The inflated fishes make attractive talking points and their preserved, spiky bodies are often seen on sale as tasteless curios where the fish are caught, laying yet another conservation problem at the door of man.

The spiny puffer can swallow so much air and water that it inflates and its spines become erect. Even if taken into a large mouth, it is impossible to swallow.

This group of fishes, found worldwide in all warm and tropical seas, have two teeth in each jaw. These are fused together to form a powerful beak.

When not inflated, pufferfishes and porcupinefishes swim gracefully, but when any kind of danger threatens they immediately swallow air or water. With the body inflated and the spines erect, they are unable to swim and float helplessly, sometimes upside-down, on the surface of the water.

Handling an inflated puffer. When the threat is past, stomach muscles cause ingested air and water to be expelled.

As well as being able to inflate themselves to deter predators, the flesh of puffers is highly toxic. This is the masked pufferfish, found in the Red Sea, covered with hundreds of small spines.

All kinds of teeth – some in unusual places

In the course of their evolution, fishes have developed a very wide range of teeth. As in all predatory animals, those fish that attack living food have large doglike teeth to grasp their prey and, in many cases, numbers of small, sharp teeth as well. The sharks, for example, are renowned for their deadly jaws, armed with huge, serrated triangular teeth. These are continuously replaced on a 'production line'; as teeth at the front of the jaws become worn or broken, new ones emerge to take their place in a matter of days. Interestingly, pikes and trout also have teeth on the tongue and in the roof of the mouth. Many fish, such as the rays, skates and wrasses, have blunt crushing and grinding teeth. The carp family have perhaps the most unusual teeth. They grow on bones in the throat and behind the gills, and are linked to the gills and gill-covers. As the gill-covers move in and out during respiration, these 'throat teeth' work against bony pads to crush and masticate plant material.

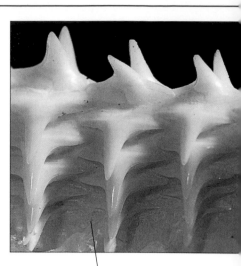

Most sharks have a never-ending supply of teeth. Their lungeing feeding habits often mean that teeth are lost or broken, but replacements are always ready to fill the gap.

Teeth evolved from scales on the lips of early fishes.

In time, the teeth became adapted to suit the feeding behaviour of the fish. The predatory barracuda, for example, have long, doglike grasping teeth, ideal for gripping the fish on which they feed. These voracious predators - some species up to 2m(6.5ft) long - roam the brightly lit upper layers of tropical and subtropical waters, using their large eyes to spot likely prey.

Parrotfishes are like the grazing cattle of the reef, constantly grinding away at the coral surfaces with their strong 'parrotlike' beaks and, in the process, turning huge amounts of coral into the white coral sand of tropical shores.

The parrotfish's incisor teeth are fused together into rounded chisels, strong enough to scrape algae from coral growths.

Carps and related fishes have additional teeth deep within the throat. The teeth are part of the bones bearing the gill rakers and as the gill-covers move in and out the teeth grind against pads in the roof of the throat, as this simple cutaway shows.

Throat teeth help to grind up plant material.

These are the throat teeth of an emperor tetra - quite different from those in the carp family.

The eel's amazing migration

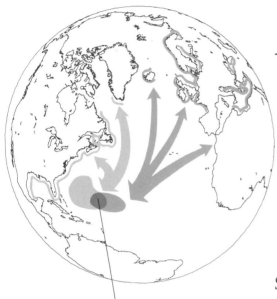

European eels spawn in the Sargasso Sea and American eels west of that area. When the European and American continents were joined millions of years ago, the eels shared a closer spawning ground and maintained it as the continents drifted apart.

At about 6mm(0.25in) long, these eel larvae are carried by ocean curents from the Sargasso Sea to inshore waters.

Aristotle, the Greek philosopher, thought that eels appeared spontaneously in mud; Pliny, a roman naturalist, told how eels appeared in slime. Hundreds of years later it was seriously suggested that if horse hair was cut into pieces and left in water, eels would be formed. Even in the nineteenth century, a book on fishes told how wet turves cut up would produce eels, or that a small beetle gave birth to young eels. In reality, the European eel's life story is much more fascinating, and it was uncovered by a Dane, Johannes Schmidt, who published his theory early in the 1900s. In reality, the eels' method of reproduction is the opposite of that of the salmon: when their time comes, eels leave fresh water and find their way to the Sargasso Sea (an area of calm water in the North Atlantic, northeast of the West Indies), where they spawn in deep water during early spring and die. The transparent leaf-shaped offspring that hatch from the eggs, once identified as a separate species of fish, take three years to travel the distance of about 4,800km(3,000 miles) back across the Atlantic, where they enter fresh water as elvers, or 'glass eels'. The elver's body must undergo considerable changes as it enters the river water.

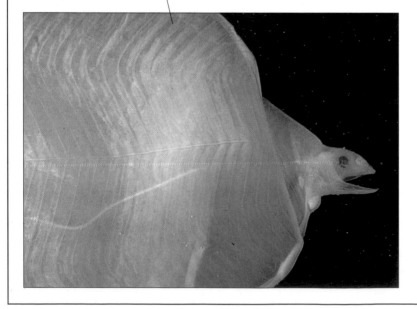

Eels live in estuaries or rivers for several years, until they become adult. The eel's migration still holds many mysteries; it may be that the European adults do not reach the Sargasso Sea and are 'replenished' by American eel larvae.

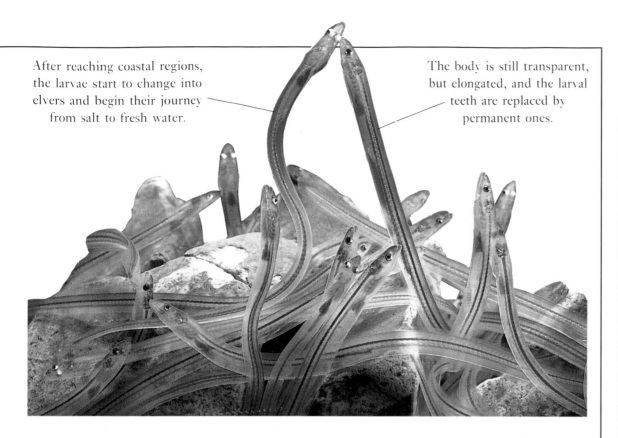

After reaching coastal regions, the larvae start to change into elvers and begin their journey from salt to fresh water.

The body is still transparent, but elongated, and the larval teeth are replaced by permanent ones.

In common with some other fishes, the eel has poor circulation, so a 'lymph heart' located in the tail pulsates and sends aerated blood into the capillaries.

❏ There are related eels with similar life histories in other parts of the world. In Australasian waters, another freshwater eel makes its spawning migration to the Pacific Ocean, while an African species deposits its eggs into the Indian Ocean. All these related eels have an intermediate stage between hatching and the adult eel.

❏ On their way to the sea, eels wriggle across country at night, usually when dew moistens the grass (as shown below). Roads prove no major obstacle to them; motorists have seen swarms of eels slithering across their path.

❏ A closely related eel living in North American rivers and ponds bordering the Atlantic Ocean makes a similar journey to the same breeding grounds as the European eel. The larvae take just one year to make the journey to the fresh waters of North America, maturing more quickly than the European eel larvae. Some scientists think that the American and European eel are the same species.

Archerfishes – shooting from the lip

Robin Hood would have been proud of the hot-shot archerfishes, for their aim is deadly accurate. Measuring barely 30cm(12in) long and found in the brackish mangrove swamps of the Indo-Pacific area where they breed, one species travels up the rivers of India and Southeast Asia to engage in its archery. This takes the form of spitting water-pellets with great accuracy at crustaceans, insects and water snails clinging to leaves or vegetation above the surface of the water. Archerfishes spit their water-bullets out so fast that they sting when they hit the skin. The fishes shoot by getting into a near vertical position, taking aim with their binocular eyes at targets 1-3m(3-10ft) away, and then turning the mouth into a tube and compressing water by contracting the gill-covers. This sends the water out in a jet that strikes the insect, knocks it into the water and into the mouth of the waiting archerfish. Of course, none of this is the result of conscious thought, but is totally based on instinctive action. The secret of success of these fishes lies in their vision through the surface film of the water. Most fishes' eyes are not adapted to accurate sight in air, and their vision through the surface layer is distorted by refraction. When an archerfish starts to lock onto a target, it approaches from immediately below, thus minimizing the distortion.

As the gills are pulled shut and the tongue makes a tube with the roof of the mouth, the archerfish creates sufficient water pressure to project a forceful stream of water droplets. The tip of the tongue helps to aim the jet.

To compensate for the effect of light refracted through water, the archerfish improves its aim by positioning itself as vertically as possible. This crucial manoeuvring is aided by good coordination between the eyes and fins.

The success of the archerfish's aim is due to its excellent binocular vision, a necessity for assessing range.

An insect on a leaf overhanging the water is a prime target for the archerfish, and will eventually be dislodged by the torrent of water droplets.

The deep, stocky body of the archerfish enables it to develop the power necessary to shoot water considerable distances, and the flat upper shape allows it to swim very close to the water surface.

Archerfishes must practise to be perfect. When young, their range is limited but, with age and experience, they can 'fire' accurate water bullets at targets up to 3m(10ft) away.

❏ The archerfishes' aim is poor when young but improves with practice! The fishes seem to polish up their skills by aiming at non-edible objects, but this may just be a case of mistaken identity!

❏ While the mechanism of the archerfishes' target practice is well understood, their breeding habits are virtually unknown. One reason for this is that they may migrate to sea to breed.

❏ The archerfishes from Thailand are eaten and also kept as petfishes. With some encouragement, and the offering of suitable food, they can be induced to display their archery skills to visitors. But leaning over the aquarium might result in an eyeful of water droplets!

❏ When their aim misses the target, archerfishes have been seen to leap out of the water and snap up flying insects or knock the overhanging vegetation so that the prey falls into the water, to be taken in the normal way.

❏ Not only is the water jet of the archer notable for its accuracy, but also for its force. Unsuspecting insect prey hit by the powerful stream of droplets have been lifted 0.3m(1ft) into the air.

❏ Deprived of suitable targets when kept in an aquarium, the archerfish will readily accept pieces of crab, shrimp, raw meat and fish in its diet.

The mussel-bound bitterling

At breeding time, the female bitterling grows an egglaying tube, or ovipositor, that may be 6cm(2.4in) long.

An old question asks: 'Which came first, the chicken or the egg?' Clearly, one could not exist without the other. The same query applies to the bitterling and the mussel. Measuring 9cm(3.5in) long and weighing less than 28gm(1oz), the bitterling spends its life among dark, dense weed patches in the slow rivers and still waters of northern and eastern Europe, feeding on plant life and small underwater creatures. Its remarkable dependence on the mussel becomes apparent at breeding time, when the female fish ejects a long, fleshy tube through which she deposits over 100 eggs into the soft mantle of the mussel. Then the male fish clouds the water with milt (sperm), which the mussel takes into the mantle through its siphon. The eggs, now fertilized, remain inside the mussel for about a month before hatching, safe from predators and bathed in well-oxygenated water. Meanwhile, the mussel has suffered no harm. And there is yet another fascinating aspect of this already astonishing story. It seems that the mussel's own breeding season is the same as that of the bitterling, April to July. When the tiny mussel larvae hatch, they attach themselves to the fish's gills. A cyst forms around each larva until their shells develop, and then the young mussels drop away from the host to begin their adult lives.

The male bitterling finds a suitable mussel and entices a passing female to join him. He will signal her to follow him by holding his tail to one side. If she is ready, the pair will lay and fertilize eggs in the mussel.

During the breeding season, the male bitterling becomes very colourful, with a red-orange belly and throat. The fins, meanwhile, adopt an attractive red tinge. Both the European bitterling and a subspecies found in China share the same unique method of reproduction.

The male and female will deposit and fertilize eggs in several batches until up to 100 are laid.

The fins maintain the fish's correct head-down position over the mussel.

The female bitterling manoeuvres her long ovipositor into the mussel's exhalant siphon and lays the eggs inside the mantle.

The host for the bitterling's eggs is the swan mussel. This bivalve can grow to 15cm(6in) or more in slow-moving water.

The male hovers intently until the ovipositor is withdrawn. Then the male will place its body close to the mussel's inhalant siphon so that the released sperm is drawn in to fertilize the eggs.

❏ The bitterling takes its name from the bitter taste of the fish, but why should this small, many-boned relative of the carp be considered desirable as food?

❏ Unlike some carps, the bitterling can expect to live no longer than five years.

❏ At spawning time, the male bitterling develops a deep blue-mauve coloration behind the head and white spots on the head, a typical response in this family of fishes.

❏ Just before the breeding season, the freshwater mussel releases a 'trigger' substance into the water that encourages the eggs inside the female bitterling to ripen.

❏ The bitterling has long been sold as an aquarium fish. If freshwater mussels are introduced into an aquarium holding bitterling, the fish become visibly excited.

❏ Fish eggs deposited on aquatic plants will die if the water level drops and they become exposed. Bitterling eggs inside the mussel are protected against this; if the water level drops, the mussel will instinctively move to deeper water and take its store of bitterling eggs with it.

❏ The lumpsucker, a sea fish, copies the bitterling's unusual style of breeding by depositing its eggs into the shell of a crab for similar protection.

Fighting with tooth and fin

A number of fishes fight in defence of their territory but, in common with the rest of the animal world, the fights are not always to the death. Instead, they have become ritualistic displays, with the 'winner' remaining to see the usually unbloodied 'loser' retreat. The exception to this is the well-known Siamese fighting fish. In Thailand, where betting is a national obsession, Siamese fighting fish are bred in large numbers. Male fish are pitted against one another and large wagers are placed on the fancied winner. When put together in a suspended glass bowl, two males adopt their most vivid coloration patterns and immediately attack each other. The fights are vicious, and severe injuries to fins are common, but the fish are not allowed to fight to the death. However, the wounds can become infected and fish die due to secondary causes. These brilliantly coloured fighting fishes are so aggressive that they attack the females and fish of other species, and have to be kept in separate containers when they are not fighting. It is possible that the battles of Siamese fighting fishes are a ritual display that has somehow got out of hand.

The male stickleback is a brave fighter. The male will defend its nest against allcomers and when the young are hatched he shepherds them about with great care and parental concern.

The splendid male Siamese fighting fishes have been bred into a wide colour range, including red, violet, blue and green.

The male's first move in the courtship ritual is a brilliant colour display from the body and fins as it circles the female fish. But should this not produce the desired result, the male turns to a fiercely aggressive display of biting and then slapping the female with its long fins. In an aquarium, it is advisable to keep a single male with one or two females. If mating succeeds, the male builds a bubble-nest at the surface and guards the 400–500 eggs.

Despite their small size, many gobies are just as pugnacious as much larger fishes. Males defend their territory by dashing out with mouth open and ready to bite.

Male Siamese fighting fishes are very aggressive and will not hesitate to fight to the death in a territorial dispute. It is vital not to keep males together.

❏ The natural diet of the Siamese fighting fish consists mostly of mosquitoes. It has been estimated that each fish eats 15,000 larvae every year.

❏ The males of fighting fishes found in Java and Sumatra incubate eggs in their mouth.

❏ At breeding time, the males of nest-building fishes face each other and fight to defend their territory, the prime example being the stickleback. The male stickleback, never more than 10cm(4in) long, adopts a vivid coloration of red belly and metallic green top and sides, and will stoutly defend the nest area, attacking fishes much larger than itself and even nipping at fingers waggled near it in the water.

❏ The marine klipfishes are a group of small, scaled blennies that sometimes fight face-to-face with their gill-covers wide open, thereby revealing their colourful false eye-spots and giving them the appearance of a much larger fish. These fights are rarely physical, the aggressive display being acted out until one fish retreats.

❏ Another klipfish appears to go into a trance if held in the hand and makes little or no attempt to wriggle free.

❏ Even among the world's smallest fish - the gobies - fighting is a part of life. In their tiny world of rocky crevices, male gobies often have fights to defend their own territory.

Swords, spears, saws and sails

Three kinds of fishes have snouts with a protruding upper jaw, the longest being that of the swordfish, in which the sword may represent up to a third of its total body length. Both the sailfish and the spearfish also have swordlike projections, but they are shorter. The most prominent part of the sailfish, as its common name suggests, is the huge cobalt–blue dorsal fin. These fishes are not to be confused with the sawfish, which also has an elongated, toothed and flattened snout, but which is a member of the shark family. Sailfishes are found in the Atlantic and Pacific Oceans and are keenly sought by anglers because of the thrilling fight they put up, leaping high into the air, their huge dorsal fins flapping and pointed snouts flailing. The sawfish does not use its saw as a weapon, even though there are many tales to the contrary. Any attack on a swimmer is more likely to be a defensive action, although for the unfortunate victim involved the resulting lacerations are bound to be painful, since there are 16-23 teeth on each side of the blade. The 'teeth' are modified skin denticles embedded in sockets, and the fish uses the saw simply to poke about on the seabed for anything edible.

The blue marlin is distributed worldwide in warm and tropical seas, The heavier blue marlins are always females, reaching over 600kg(1,300lb).

The pale lines down the flanks of the striped marlin give it its name. Marlins, swordfish and members of the sailfish family are among the fastest swimmers in the open ocean, reaching speeds of 100kph(62mph).

Blue marlin take squid and octopus, but prefer tuna and bonito, and have even being found with young swordfish in their stomachs.

The sawshark uses its extended upper jaw to probe sediments for small fish and other creatures, and may stun them with side swipes.

The crescent-shaped tail of the sailfish shows it to be a fast-moving ocean predator.

The huge dorsal fin of the sailfish would certainly deter potential predators from trying to swallow the fish. Evidence suggests that it may use the erected dorsal fin to herd prey fish into a shoal before swiming through them with its jaws snapping.

When newly hatched, this handsome fish is no more than 3mm(0.8in) long. At 20cm(8in), it shows all the features of the adult, including the extended upper jaw.

❏ While it has been known to wound prey fish or stun them with its sword, the swordfish's rapier-like snout seems merely to be the result of streamlining taken to the extreme.

❏ Do fishes feel pain? This question has been asked many times and not satisfactorily answered. But after being played on rod and line for some hours, one swordfish proceeded to swim up to and feed on prey fish.

❏ Many people who have never seen a whole swordfish have enjoyed steaks cut from the body of this handsome and powerful creature. It feeds on many deepwater fish, as well as on squid, and because of its strength it has few predators. Among these are sharks; one mako shark killed off the Bahamas and dissected was found to have eaten a 53kg(120lb) swordfish.

❏ Reaching 6m(20ft) long and weighing over 46kg(1,100lb), the swordfish is a formidable creature. Old sailors' tales tell of a swordfish hurling itself at wooden boats and piercing the side with its sword so that the craft sank. One account tells of a swordfish driving its sword into a ship with a force that would have needed ten blows of a 9kg(30lb) hammer. Another report describes a sword being driven through a ship's copper sheathing, 10cm(4in) of hard wood, 30cm(12in) of solid oak and finally penetrating an oil cask!

SUPERFACTS

Man's distant fishy relations

If fishes with backbones had not evolved, it is highly possible that man would not exist in his present form. A clue to man's watery ancestry is his prenatal existence in the womb, where the embryo lives in an entirely liquid environment, with gills very like the gill pouches of the fish embryo. They do not develop into gill slits as they do in an adult fish, however, nor do they develop gill membranes. Later in the gestation period, they become modified and the human embryo eventually takes nourishment from the mother's own bloodstream.

Scaly ladies ▲

The mermaid above was depicted on the 13th-century Clonfert Cathedral, County Galway, Eire. In the days when voyages to far-off lands took years, most spent out of sight of land, anything remotely resembling a woman was bound to fire a sailor's imagination. Tales of mermaids spread until, in the 17th century, scientists decided that all mermaid sightings were of dugongs (sea cows). Sir James Emerson Tennant wrote, 'If disturbed, the dugong dives under water and tosses up her fishlike tail.'

A fish out of water ▲

The nimble mudskipper spends much of its time hopping about on the mudflats of the African, Asian and Australian swamps. This amphibious fish is able to live out of water by retaining water in its gill chambers and extracting oxygen from it. The mudskipper can replenish its supply from a pool or puddle and can also absorb air through the skin, as well as through the lining of the mouth and pharynx. On land their all-round vision is important for spotting predators. The eyes are on pods that can be rotated in all directions. There are no tear ducts, so if the eyeball dries out it is lowered and lubricated. To move along, the nimble mudskipper swings its pectoral fins forward and supports its body weight on the pelvic fins. As if on crutches, the body is drawn forward and up and then falls back down again.

The biggest flatfish

The halibut is easily the biggest flatfish, growing to enormous weights of over 360kg(700lb). It is found only in the cold waters of the North Atlantic and feeds on fish, squid, octopus and crustaceans. The female halibut deposits some two million eggs in deep water, which hatch into 7mm(0.27in)-long larvae that soon move down to the seabed.

Dangerous fish

All sharks should be considered dangerous, even the carpet sharks - a lethargic and tasselled group of Australian fishes called wobbegongs by the Aborigines. Although not thought to be dangerous, one took hold of a swimmer's leg and, even though its body was penetrated by a spear, refused to let go of its victim.

What the scales tell

Many fish species, especially those in the large cyprinid family, can be identified by the shape of their flexible rounded scales. But this is not all. The age of the fish can be estimated closely by counting the concentric growth rings that develop on the scales, and these also give an idea of the general health of the fish. The best scales for this purpose are those from the 'shoulder', not from the flanks.

Frozen fish

On record is a hailstone, said to be as large as a hen's egg, that fell in Germany in 1806. As it melted, it was found to contain a tiny crucian carp measuring 40mm(1.6in).

When man meets fish

The invention of the aqualung has allowed man to re-enter and explore the underwater world of fishes, his ancestral home.

The smallest fish

The pygmy goby is not only the smallest fish but also the smallest vertebrate. A fully grown adult pygmy goby can grow to 11mm(0.43in) long, but mature specimens have been measured at 7.5mm(0.3in).

Tiny predators

Although they measure only 2.5cm(1in) long, the tusked gobies have relatively large, curved canine teeth. These fish have made their homes inside sponges in the Caribbean sea, and it is thought that their 'tusks' enable them to force their way through the sponges' narrow internal passages.

The largest fish ▲

The whale shark is the largest fish in the world. It is known to reach a length of 12m(40ft) and can weigh about 20.3 tonnes (44,750lb). Despite its huge size, it does not present a threat to humans, because it feeds on tiny crustaceans called krill. On his Kon Tiki expedition, Thor Heyerdahl's raft was followed by a huge but friendly whale shark.

Long distance smell

Sharks compensate for poor eyesight by a keen sense of smell. They can detect just a few molecules of blood at huge distances and home in on prey.

SUPERFACTS

Shark on toast?

When a hammerhead shark is netted and killed in Iceland, the carcass is buried in the semi-frozen ground for periods of up to six months. After that it is dug up and the dark-pink, close-textured flesh is cut up and eaten like cheese. Similarly, Greenland shark meat is poisonous if eaten fresh, but wholesome when part decayed. This is a very long-lived, slow-growing shark. One 25cm(10in) specimen was tagged and when recaptured after 16 years, had only grown 7.5cm(3in).

The largest freshwater fish

A swim in a quiet stream somewhere in South America, possibly the Amazon, might be interrupted by a meeting with a 4m(13ft)-long fish called the arapaima. This, with the beluga, is the largest freshwater fish, reaching 200kg(440lb) and, like the whale shark, is not known for its speed and agility. The arapaima lives in waters that can be oxygen-poor and has developed its swimbladder to act as a temporary lung, as well as an organ of balance. Interestingly, it has a few relatives, one in African and another in Asian fresh water, all on the same parallel. If the continents were joined, the waters where these fishes are found would be close together. Evidence of this kind has confirmed the theory of continental drift. ▼

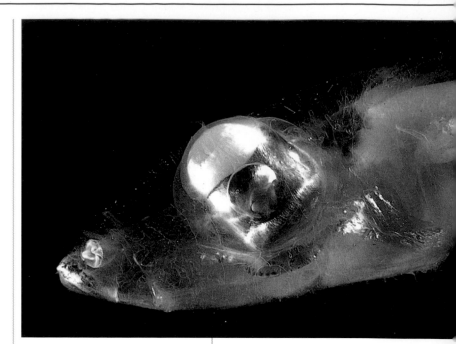

Elaborate nests

One of the most elaborate nests is constructed by the familiar little stickleback. The male scoops out a depression and deposits plant material in the hole. Having piled up pieces of weed, he creates a tunnel through the mound and then swims back and forth over the nest, releasing a secretion from the kidneys that binds the structure together. The female is then induced to enter the tunnel and deposit her eggs, after which she swims off, leaving the male to bring up the family.

The male labyrinth fish blows bubbles into a blob of mucus to form a floating nest at the water surface. The eggs float up into this raft of bubbles and the male assumes responsibility until they hatch.

Deepwater fish ▲

No swimmer will ever meet the fish shown above, for it lives 1,000m(3,300ft) down in the blackness of the tropical Atlantic and eastern Pacific. Deepwater probes have seen and described them, but few of these surprisingly small and little-understood bathyspheric fishes have common names. The eyes of *Dolichopteryx* are on stalks and can see upwards and sideways at the same time - but in the total blackness of the depths of the sea what use is binocular vision to this fish?

Fish move in mysterious ways

Since 70 percent of the surface of the earth is covered by water, it is not surprising that many fishes make migrations either for feeding or reproduction. The factor that has made many migrations mysterious, is the often huge distances over which fish can swim. Bluefin tuna, for example, migrate 4,800km (3,000 miles) after spawning in the Caribbean Sea.

What's in a name?

Depending on where one is, the same fish species can have very different common names. The European cyprinids - roach, dace and so on, are called minnows in the USA, whereas in Europe the minnow is a small shoaling fish. There are trout in Australian seas that are not 'real' trout, but reef fishes. Salmon-bass often figure on restaurant menus, but no such fish exist; the dish is probably sea trout or bass. The salmon-shark found in the Pacific is neither salmon nor shark, but a member of the mackerel family. Many of the exotically named 'trout' in US rivers are not true trouts at all. The brook and lake trouts are charrs, and the cutthroat, kamloops, shasta and steelhead are nearer to the salmon family. Until very recently, the rainbow was officially a trout and its migratory form was called the steelhead. Now, however, both rainbow and steelhead have been included in the family of Pacific salmon because of their habitat.

Fish that didn't hear the bell

Travellers have often been told that fish kept in monastery ponds or castle moats would come to be fed if a bell was rung over the water. Visitors would dutifully bring food, ring the bell and up came the fish. On one occasion, the clapper fell off, the bell did not ring, but up came the fish! It was then realized that the sound had never been heard by the fish, but they had responded to the movement of the bell, which was clearly visible from beneath the water surface. The fish had become accustomed to this activity heralding the arrival of food.

Roman fishermen

The Romans knew of the culinary delights to be had from fish and netted them in huge quantities. But they also followed the 'get-away-from-it-all' pleasures of angling, and their mosaics give detailed pictures of the sea and freshwater fishes, as well as the crustaceans and molluscs with which they were familiar. Like Izaak Walton in the mid-seventeenth century, the Romans used long hairs from the tails of white stallions for lines and, again like him, had no winch or reel, tying the line directly to the end of a cane rod. One of the Romans' favourite fish was the mullet, but they also netted trout and, albeit with reluctance, ate pike. ▼

A population explosion

The manmade Kariba Lake in Zambia, Africa, holds a huge number of cichlids that have found ecological niches in which to thrive. One species has even developed perchlike jaws and become predatory. As a result of this species explosion - unknown in fish studies - we have a unique opportunity to understand how evolution works.

Tell me when it hurts

The question 'do fish feel pain?' has exercised the minds of many fish scientists. To a human being 'pain', which is the body's way of warning us about physical damage, varies from the nuisance pinprick to unbearable agony. This is due to the complexity of the human nervous system, but will a fish, with its much simpler nervous system, experience variations of pain? Perhaps the answer lies in the apocryphal report of an angler who accidentally hooked a pike in the eye, removing the eye entirely. The angler left this gruesome bait on the hook, only to catch the same one-eyed fish again. The conclusion was that if the pike was still able to feed, it could not be in great pain.

Unlucky butterfish

The butterfish, also known as the gunnel, belongs to a group of inshore fishes, most of which act as intermediate hosts to the parasites that infest seabirds. Near seabird colonies, the unfortunate butterfish is often completely covered in black spots. These are the sites of encysted larvae of a parasitic worm that attacks the birds.

SUPERFACTS

The hidden predator ▲
The oddly named John Dory might be regarded as the 'stealth' fish, for with its very narrow body it is able to approach food fish virtually unseen. Then its protractile mouth comes into play, the jaws strike rapidly forward and the meal is swallowed. Known as *Zeus faber* in Europe and *Zeus ocellata* in the US, its scientific name must have some religious connection. It is said that the large black spots, one on each flank, represent the thumb and forefinger prints of St. Peter. The common name may derive from French *jaune* for yellow.

A leap into the unknown
The frillfin goby, found on both sides of the tropical Atlantic, explores rock pools at high tide. As one pool is isolated by the receding tide, the goby jumps unerringly into another, even if it cannot see where it is going.

A specialized feeder
The Malawi eye-biter certainly lives up to its name. It attacks other fish and bites out their eyes with specialized teeth in the lower jaw. It also has the unusual habit of swallowing whole prey tail-first. Other cichlids in the African Rift Valley Lakes have evolved particular feeding patterns, involving scale-scraping or capturing young fish from the parent's mouth. *Melanochromis vermivorus* in Lake Malawi eats nothing but aquatic worms. It is perch- or pikelike in shape.

The isolated antipodes
Although they occur on such a large continent, the rivers and lakes of Australia have only two indigenous true freshwater fishes. They are the descendants of primitive species, such as the lungfish, and species of osteoglossid fishes found in North Australia and New Guinea. Some species have no common name. Man has introduced game fishes, such as the brown and rainbow trout and cyprinids (carp-type fish). There is one Australian freshwater eel known as the short-finned species.

Suffering sticklebacks
Fishes can suffer from a wide variety of diseases and parasites. One of these - the tapeworm - can multiply in the body cavity of a small fish. A 2.5cm(1in)-long stickleback was found to be host to 72 tapeworm larvae. Not surprisingly, its body was grossly deformed.

Diet deficiency can lead to bone diseases in fish. The vertebrae become distorted and the result is a fish with a lateral curved spine. In an indoor aquarium, where fish are not exposed to ultraviolet light, they may suffer from a lack of vitamins A and D.

Lethal teeth ▼

A great white shark tooth from a modern shark is compared here with a huge example from an ancient ancestor. The jaws of the old shark are so large that six men can sit easily between them, and the fish would have been at least 24m(80ft) long. The power behind the jaws of the great white shark has been well publicized in shark documentaries and *that* film. The large, serrated, triangular teeth are so sharp that sailors have been known to shave with them. This lethal cutting edge is coupled with the fish's habit of clamping the jaws into a chunk of fresh meat and worrying the head from side to side. The jaws remain locked together until the hunk of meat is sliced away - a very efficient mode of eating. The great white was made famous by a market gardener named Alfred Dean. While fishing off South Australia, he caught six great white shark, all over 1 tonne (2,200lb) in weight. They can be dangerous even when apparently lifeless. One scientist unthinkingly put his hand between the jaws of a great white shark that had been disembowelled - and the fish's jaws clamped shut and bit off the man's hand.

Mysterious depths ▲

The depths of the oceans hold fishes that are often extremely grotesque to our eyes. The rattails, also more romantically called grenadiers, are one group. All have large heads, a short body and a thin, tapering scaly tail from which they take their name. The eyes of animals that live in places where light, if any, is at a minimum are either very large or have atrophied. These fishes have large eyes, perhaps in order to see the luminous patterns of other fishes, possibly as part of their mating display. Much of their lifestyle is as yet unknown.

An unlikely pair

The Californian arrow goby spends its life near the burrow of a ghost shrimp. When hatched, the goby has eyes, but they cease to function as the fish matures, and it depends on the shrimp for food, nibbling off debris that it leaves behind. If danger threatens, the goby darts into the burrow, thus warning the shrimp, which follows the fish to safety. If the shrimp dies, the goby must find another host or perish.

A mouthful from mother

The mouthbrooding cichlids are a fascinating group of fishes. At spawning time, the male creates a depression in the bottom sediment into which the female deposits her eggs. The male fertilizes them and then the waiting female scoops the eggs into her mouth, where they remain until they hatch, safe from predation. Once hatched, the fry leave the mother's mouth and swim freely, although during the early days the young fry retreat back into their mother's mouth when danger threatens. Both the male and female of the Galilee cichlid have been known to hold over 1,200 eggs in their mouths. Mouthbrooding cichlids do not food while carrying eggs and fry, but some unfortunate young may be swallowed.

Both sexes of the discus fish from South America hold fry in their mouths for protection, but after about three days the young move away and then cling to their parents' bodies, feeding on the slimy covering for five weeks and ignoring other food. A pair of discus fishes, also known for good reason as pompadour fishes, are among the most attractive aquarium inhabitants.

INDEX

This is the queen angelfish, from Florida, the Bahamas and south to the coast of Brazil. This is a juvenile, showing the vertical blue markings that will disappear in the adult fish. Many juvenile reef fishes have more complex patterns than the adults, presumably to disguise them against their dappled background.

A flatfish of the 'eyes to the left' group, which includes the turbot, brill and the oddly named Eckstrom's topknot. Flatfishes with 'eyes to the right' include the halibut and the dab. All flatfishes begin life as upright fishes but spend their adult lives lying on one side.

The predatory redtail catfish devours crustaceans, invertebrates and other fish.

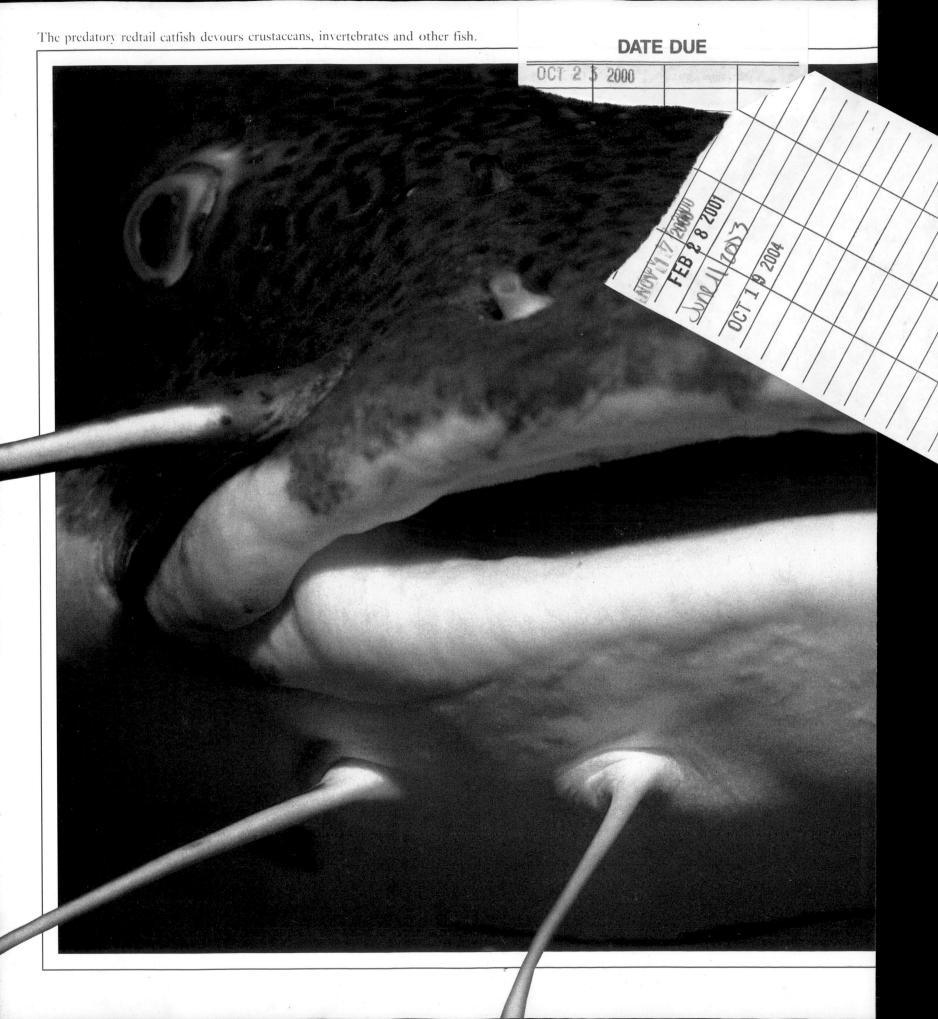

The predatory redtail catfish devours crustaceans, invertebrates and other fish.